Creating a HAVEN of Peace

What People Are Saying about
Creating a HAVEN of Peace

"There's a lot to love about Joanne Miller's new book. What I love most is her conviction that our choices matter. Life happens—and sometimes in ways that hurt. But, as her own story demonstrates, we can choose to respond to the difficult times in ways that don't add hurt upon hurt, but rather restore and heal."

—**Michael Hyatt**, *New York Times* bestselling author of *Platform*

"This world can be a pretty crazy place, and we can always use a little more peace—especially in our homes. In Creating a Haven of Peace, our good friend Joanne Miller offers some great practical ideas for creating genuine, God-honoring peace under your roof. We've watched Joanne practice these principles for decades. They work for her, and we know they'll work for you, too."

—**Sharon and Dave Ramsey**

"Haven of peace is a perfect description of Joanne and Dan's home. A rare commodity in today's world. We want our grandchildren to experience that treasure. We are using her book to transform our home."

—**Diane and Ken Davis**, motivational speaker, author of *Fully Alive*

"Joanne Miller embodies this message more than anyone I can think of. And not just to family or house guests. She creates a haven of peace, love, acceptance, and fun wherever she goes. In her home. At her events. On her property. Out and about. Wherever she is. The world needs this message. The world needs this book."

—**Gail Hyatt**, artist and speaker

Creating
a
HAVEN
of
Peace

When You're Feeling Down,
Finances Are Flat, and Tempers are Rising

Joanne Fairchild Miller

New York

Creating a HAVEN of Peace

When You're Feeling Down, Finances Are Flat, and Tempers are Rising

Published in New York, New York, by Morgan James Publishing. Morgan James and The Entrepreneurial Publisher are trademarks of Morgan James, LLC.
www.MorganJamesPublishing.com

The Morgan James Speakers Group can bring authors to your live event. For more information or to book an event visit The Morgan James Speakers Group at
www.TheMorganJamesSpeakersGroup.com.

Shelfie

A **free** eBook edition is available
with the purchase of this print book.

CLEARLY PRINT YOUR NAME ABOVE IN UPPER CASE

Instructions to claim your free eBook edition:
1. Download the Shelfie app for Android or iOS
2. Write your name in **UPPER CASE** above
3. Use the Shelfie app to submit a photo
4. Download your eBook to any device

ISBN 978-1-63047-771-4 paperback
ISBN 978-1-63047-772-1 eBook
Library of Congress Control Number:
2015914692

Cover Design by:
Rachel Lopez
www.r2cdesign.com

Interior Design by:
Bonnie Bushman
The Whole Caboodle Graphic Design

In an effort to support local communities and raise awareness and funds, Morgan James Publishing donates a percentage of all book sales for the life of each book to Habitat for Humanity Peninsula and Greater Williamsburg.

Get involved today, visit
www.MorganJamesBuilds.com

Habitat
for Humanity®
Peninsula and
Greater Williamsburg
Building Partner

I dedicate this book to Irene and Jerry Hall

Two dear friends, who believed in us, gave Dan his first real taste of entrepreneurialism that actually brought in a paycheck, laughed with us, played with us, cried with us, and loved us through some difficult times. Jerry, you and Dan made a great team and you taught him a lot (*most of it was good!*) Irene, you and I will always be there for one another. We understand our men and we know for a fact they would be lost without us! I thought of you often as I wrote these pages.

And to Dan, Kevin, Jared, and Ashley

There is no greater love on this earth than the love I have for you four.

Table of Contents

Disclaimer

I'm going to be real with you. Rather than have a lot of legal terminology and disclaimers I will just say plainly that I do not have letters after my name. I am simply Joanne Fairchild Miller. I don't have certifications, degrees, and credentials. I'm not apologizing for that because I earned a doctorate in Marriage and Family just as valid as any college degree or certification (if not more so). Not by regurgitating facts and formulas from a textbook but from the reality of life experience. I had a lot of teachers. Mentors who shared their successes with me through conversations, books, videos, conferences, and simply by example. People I looked to for help from how to love unconditionally to how to incorporate beauty in my life. I learned a lot about what I didn't want; the marriages I had seen in my past and the ones I have seen along the way in couples who sacrifice family for career. So, when reading the pages ahead, remember I am just like many of you. A person who drew a line in the sand and said, *Not me! Not my marriage and not my home!* A person who worked hard to create a Haven of Peace in spite of circumstances and in spite of the sacrifices and the labor intensity. This is what worked for us and my hope is you will find examples you want to emulate to create your own Haven of Peace. It's never too late!

A Note from Joanne

This is a compilation of articles, blogs, quotations and thoughts on home and family that I have been writing and sharing with others for over twenty years. At the time I began to put pencil to paper (I actually started out that way!), I had been married enough years to garner considerable positive experience so that others looking at my life, at our peaceful home, began asking how we managed to create our Haven of Peace. In my first attempts to put my thoughts on paper, I had titled this book, *Creating a Haven of Peace ... In a Broken World*. Indeed, we do live in a broken world. With all the chaos and busyness around us, all the noise and confusion, all the anger and frustration, it can be difficult to create a peaceful refuge where one can escape and find sanctuary. My desire is not to draw attention to all the negatives in our environment, but instead to give positive examples of what has worked for us and why others are curious as to how we have created the life we want.

Many years ago my husband, Dan, and I were greatly impacted by the classic movie, *The Hunchback of Notre Dame*, based on the 1831 novel by Victor Hugo. The rather ugly and grotesque Quasimodo was taunted, beaten, and treated very badly, but whenever he escaped and went to the Cathedral (Notre Dame), he would yell, *"Sanctuary!"* and would receive asylum there. Through the years, Dan and I have felt strongly that everyone needs a sanctuary where they feel safe, comforted, and loved.

This is what we have worked hard to provide for our children and now our grandchildren. But our desire to create a sanctuary has touched lives far beyond our own family. In the year 2000, we came out of a valley of financial debt and inability to own a home and into God's provision of the home where we currently reside. There is a wonderful story about how this happened and how blessed we felt, but most important to this story is that we knew without a doubt God had provided this acreage for us to bless others. To create the Haven of Peace we had longed for, worked hard for, and envisioned in our hearts. To create a **Sanctuary**.

Make it your goal to create a marriage
that feels like the safest place on earth.
—**Greg Smalley, Focus on the Family**

Did you know that Sanctuary is also where immunity is granted? We believe love in the home should be unconditional. No matter how serious someone's offense, a true Sanctuary provides asylum, love, and immunity. Not condemnation or anger or unforgiveness.

Our home reflects this peace and safety for anyone who enters. But we also have another Sanctuary (by that name) on our property. We acquired an old barn that has become a popular place for our events, parties, and for housing guests. We did a lot of revamping to make it a comfortable place where guests and friends come for the refreshment of mind, body, and soul. Besides the events we hold there, we also have weekly art classes that our group often calls "church." It is not unusual for us to feel a sense of spiritual awakening within the walls of that old barn. Dan's office is there and his desire is that anyone who enters feels that spirit of unconditional acceptance and love.

> Where we love is home—home that
> our feet may leave but not our hearts.
> —**Oliver Wendell Holmes**

But the story didn't begin with the acquisition of the beautiful nine acres we have in Franklin, Tennessee. We didn't wait for our circumstances to be perfect to begin the quest for peace in our home. In fact, it all started back on March 23, 1968, when two became one. We vowed to love one another "… for better, for worse, for richer or poorer, in sickness and in health, to love and to cherish, 'til death do us part."* Today that may sound old-fashioned, but that's the day we drew a line in the sand and set out to add a whole new branch to our family trees. That's the day we vowed, not only our love and commitment to one another but also to be intentional about creating our Haven of Peace.

Our home was far from perfect, but it was and is a Sanctuary … a place of peace for anyone who enters… I hope you find ideas and traditions you can implement in your own home to create the peace and loving atmosphere you desire. You really can create the life you want, but you have to do it intentionally.

This wooden wall hanging was lovingly carved by Dan in the early 1970's. It has been a prominent piece of art in all the many homes we have had.

---

*   From *The Book of Common Prayer*, traditional wedding vows

Post Script … Before you start with the mental eye rolls while reading this, thinking our home was different and we lived a charmed life (yes, we have been accused of that). And you think I wouldn't understand your life, let me state quite clearly that not every day in our home was perfect. Our lives were not perfect. We struggled financially … for many, many years; through a child with drug and alcohol addictions … for a decade. We struggled with medical issues … a diagnosis of Multiple Sclerosis for me in 2000. We struggled with extended family issues. We struggled with the same kinds of disagreements and frustrations that many of you reading this book have experienced or are currently experiencing. But our goal was to create the life we wanted and it took a lot of **determination, intention, and focus**. It took a lot of work and believing we could do it even when it didn't seem possible. Sometimes we got discouraged. But we had a goal in mind and looking back I don't regret all we did to accomplish what we set out to do.

Our job isn't over by any means. I'll always be Mom. I'll always be Dan's "Babe." We will continue to have disagreements, frustrations, and occasionally even some temporary chaos. But one thing I know for sure: the threads of love, respect, honor, trust, integrity, and support will weave together to blanket our family with peace because that is what we most desire. And we are willing to sacrifice selfishness and self-absorption to achieve it. I hope the words that follow will guide you to create your own Haven of Peace.

Regardless of your past,
your tomorrow is a clean slate.
—Zig Ziglar

A Letter to My Husband: An Act of Love

Here is a letter to my husband, whose love is expressed in more ways than words. My life has been a great adventure with you as my partner. As Jerry McGuire wisely said, "You complete me!"

It is a beautiful, sun-filled autumn day and you are outside sitting on the grass, - hairdryer in one hand and a delicate crocheted doily in the other. Diligently you work at each cobweb strand of intricate threads carefully aiming the heat of the hairdryer to melt pools of thick crimson candle wax. Last night's peaceful family get-together concluded with a half-hearted effort to clean up piles of candle wax meandering thread-like amidst the delicate doily, the dried roses from our anniversary tenderly tied together with ribbon, and the family photos. I was too tired to give the mess much attention, but you noticed it first thing this morning.

After a brief discussion to ascertain how important the doily was and whether or not it was salvageable, you are now sitting in the grass painstakingly trying to melt the wax away from the handiwork. It isn't an expensive doily. In fact, I believe I picked it up for pennies at a long-ago garage sale. You have seen it in various places of ornamentation throughout the house for years. It isn't valuable but you know I like it. You can tell by my reaction to the candle mess that I am disappointed the doily may be ruined.

So you are sitting in the grass on this beautiful day making a very memorable and extensive deposit into our relational bank account. I did not ask you to touch the doily. I didn't pitch a fit or cry when the accident happened, yet you intuitively recognize that I am disappointed the accident may have destroyed something I care about. Therefore, you are lovingly and seemingly without second thought giving me a gift much more important and long-lasting than a simple doily. By your efforts, you are saying in your own language that you love me and if I am unhappy or disappointed, you will willingly take the time to try to rectify the situation.

How many times over the years have you made similar deposits in our relationship? Too numerous to count. You show me in ways that make me feel cherished, pampered, and secure. Often words are never uttered. They are incidental to the actions carried out. For these reasons I love you and for these reasons I know, beyond doubt, that I am loved.

There Are Many Ways to Say "I Love You"

On March 23, 1999, Dan and I were to celebrate our 31st anniversary and I had worked hard for months to create the perfect gift for him. I had been jotting down ways he says *"I love you"* without really saying it. Have you ever thought of that in your own relationship?

One of our favorite family movies is *Fiddler on the Roof* and I especially like the song Tevye sings to Golde when he repeatedly asks, *"Do You Love Me?"* Golde thinks about this and then recounts all the ways she has served him in the twenty-five years of their married life. *"If that's not love, what is?"* When Tevye asks her again, *"Then you love me?"* When Golde confirms, they both sing together about how nice it is to know ... even after twenty-five years.

The song brings up many ways they show their love to one another, but they find it difficult to actually attribute their actions to the concept of love. One gets the impression they had seldom or never said those **three very important words** to one another.

I recall a time in the first year of our marriage when I had a similar conversation with Dan (but it wasn't set to music!) because I so wanted him to assure me with words … often … that he loved me. He quickly pointed out to me that he worked hard to show me he loved me so why was I upset? I told him it wasn't enough for him to parrot after me when I said I love you, but I needed him to say it voluntarily, spontaneously, and often. I needed that reassurance. In those first years of marriage saying I love you often is important. But what about decades later?

On that anniversary, I wanted to express to Dan that I didn't take for granted all he does for me. That I notice. That I care deeply and I want our children to know by my writing Dan is a good husband and our love will never grow stale or apathetic. Even after decades and we are old and gray.

My skills on the computer were sadly lacking back then, but I fancied up the pages as best I could and put them together in book form, tied by yarn. I titled it *For This I Love You*. It was full of stories of how he shows me love. It contained many one- or two-line examples such as:

You respect me enough to say
"please" and "thank you" and "excuse me."
For this, I love you.

You turn on my lamp and my side of the
electric blanket before I get to bed.
For this, I love you.

You continually want to know
how to love me better.
For this, I love you.

Date night was always a high priority.
It is on your weekly schedule as an appointment
and you rarely ever break it.
For this, I love you.

You help me always to put my best foot forward
and never chastise when I fail.
We both make mistakes.
For this, I love you.

You fill my car with gas because
you know I hate to do it.
For this, I love you.

You end every phone conversation with me
and with each of our children with, "I love you!"
For this, I love you.

I could go on and on. I had lots of examples. Needless to say, Dan was very touched by this gesture of love on my part. But it was an expression that touched more people than I expected. Our children were in awe of what I had done and how Dan's actions had manifested such love, respect, and gratitude. Years later, we were to go on a business cruise over Valentine's Day. Our theme centered around relationship and we had other speakers besides us to talk on this subject. I decided to hire a graphic designer to put my little booklet together and include more stories. I printed enough to give one to each of the couples in our small group of cruisers. The resulting comments helped me know I had hit on a topic of importance. My book helped others to think about their own relationships. My intended desire was to encourage others not to take for granted the myriad ways love is shown. Not always in words but in ways that garner respect and gratitude and result in a *long-lasting, deeply fulfilling, and loving partnership.*

Love Well is about sacrificial engagement.
It is simply putting the needs of the other person in the relationship above your own.
Love Well requires short-term sacrifice for long-term gain.
It is often the opposite of "That was easy."
—**Susie Albert Miller,** *Listen, Learn, Love* **(Dunham Books, 2015)**

Chapter One

In the Beginning ...
I Had a Choice to Make

It would be hard to write a book on how intentional I have been in creating a Haven of Peace without first giving a prelude to what, perhaps, made this life-long quest high on my list of life goals. No one comes into marriage without some baggage. Some have such heavy baggage that it takes years of therapy to unload it all. Interestingly, I wasn't even aware I had much baggage 'til long after I was married, had children, and faced an empty nest. At that point, in my early 50s, I really took the time to evaluate who I was; what I brought to the table as a human being. I hadn't had much time to think about it before. I was far too busy taking care of everyone around me; feeling if I wasn't strong for everyone and making their lives easy and happy, I was not doing my job properly. Through some intense therapy and soul searching, I discovered I didn't know how to be happy except when

I made others around me happy. I didn't know how to just be me. To be happy on my own.

Life isn't about finding yourself.
Life is about creating yourself.
—George Bernard Shaw

On a trip to Chicago soon after our last child left home for college, my husband, Dan, made a statement revealing a truth that hit me like a sledgehammer. I love Chicago at Christmas. It is truly magical. But everything I saw ... the twinkling lights, the carolers, the window treatments, the light falling snow ... found me exclaiming, "Oh, I wish the kids were here to see this!" Finally, Dan asked me, "Can't you enjoy anything without the kids? Can't you enjoy it for us? For you?" I realized he was pointing out a very valid fact. I simply didn't know how to enjoy my life without seeing it through the excitement of other people's lives. It was a pattern I had a hard time breaking. It took a few years of introspection, counseling, reading, and a concerted effort to discover who I truly was and how God had uniquely prepared me for the life I was to live.

So a little personal history might give a bit of insight into why this quest for creating peace and harmony in my home became so important to me. From the first year of my married life, I knew I didn't want to emulate the chaos, anger, and unrest I had experienced growing up. But, I don't think I realized 'til well into my marriage that I had this relentless desire for Creating a Haven of Peace no matter how hard it seemed at the time. I wanted so much more than I had experienced. I hope this insight will help you look at yourself and your life with new eyes to gain a new perspective.

Will the *Real* Joanne Please Stand Up?

> Your perspective is a choice, and it plays a pivotal role in the
> reality you create around you.
> —**Jared Angaza,** *Wisdom Meets Passion*

By the time I was four years old, my mother had been divorced twice. I had two younger sisters whom I was expected to help raise … I became like a surrogate spouse, fulfilling many household duties, rarely having time to pursue activities I wanted to do. I would escape in the pages of a book as often as I could get away from the continual chores and duties I was forced to do. We lived in poverty and on welfare much of my growing up years. I was expected to clean, cook, iron, and babysit from my earliest memories. My mother was independent, domineering, and hated men. All extended family members were also divorced so there were no male influences in my life except for a step-grandfather who was distant and often drunk. My mother took out much of her frustration and anger on her children by abusive beatings and hair pulling, foul language and threats … yet her puritanical morals were strictly enforced. Thus, I was very limited in what I could do socially and outside the home. We did not attend church or clubs or other community events. We often moved so I rarely had long-term friends. My world was very narrow.

When I was seventeen, my mother remarried my father to use his money to save her home from foreclosure. Then she divorced him again after much fighting and drunken episodes in front of us children. When I was eighteen, my boyfriend (now my husband) moved me out of the house and into a rented bedroom in the home of an elderly lady.

He felt my mother had become so angry and abusive I was in harm's way. I was chronically ill with colitis and anemia due to the stress. For ten years after I married at age nineteen, my mother would make me so ill by her rages when I would visit that we vowed never to live in the same state with her. When I wanted to share the joy and excitement over the birth of our first baby, she returned my letters and pictures unopened, which crushed my heart and wounded me deeply. I longed for her approval and love.

What you have just read is one version of my story. It is true and would be a good excuse for giving up, settling for a mediocre life, and becoming a life-long victim. But here is another version of my story. I like this one better. It, too, is true. It shows a perspective I prefer to embrace and has defined my adult life far more than the prior story.

I grew up experiencing homemade clothes my grandmother lovingly put together for me and Christmases with beautiful handmade gifts and dolls. When I was entering fourth grade, my mother decided she wanted to get off welfare so she applied to college and was accepted even though she only had a tenth-grade education. We were privileged to live on the college campus and I was able to use the library often. When my mother took classes, I often studied along with her and learned about geology, English literature, science, classical music, and art. I was able to go to a small private grade school with the children of the professors at the college. I learned French in fourth grade. I had an extensive geological rock collection that I was able to put in shows. I learned how to make beautiful rock gardens. I was introduced very early to the advantages of learning and avid reading that transported me to places I had never known about before and longed to visit. I learned to make things beautiful by being creative and striving to keep my world clean of clutter and filth. I would transplant the flowers from the woods to our small patch of dirt around the Quonset hut we lived in. I learned to cook, clean, iron, and be a good housekeeper from the time I was old enough to hold a broom. I learned how to improvise and can fix just about anything with Scotch tape, rubber bands, and thumbtacks!

Because we moved often, I learned to make friends easily and to be flexible. Being the oldest in a single family home, I learned to keep house and nurture my younger sisters when my mother was too busy. My history set the stage for teaching me what I wanted for my future and what I knew I didn't want to emulate. My upbringing gave me the determination to create a Haven of Peace. My upbringing set the stage for my enjoyment of mothering and being a homemaker; to be proud of the strength I derived from not having everything given to me easily.

You can determine who you want to become and what will define your life. You can use your past as an excuse for failure or you can use it to draw a line in the sand and change your family tree.

Here's a challenge for you: Write two versions of your own story. It is a great exercise and will make you think about your own perspective and what defines you. Be as complete and descriptive as you can. Which story do you most want to continue? What legacy do you want to leave for your children that will give them a good beginning for their own story?

Creating a healthy story could change the way you see your life and the way others see and respond to you.
—**Dan Miller,** *Wisdom Meets Passion*

Two Worlds Colliding

"This couple never had a chance in marriage because they were two different worlds colliding!" Dan and I were sitting in a front pew listening to our pastor as he

Me with Dan's parents and sister, Marti, 1972.

said these words with passion. He went on to say the couple had no chance for a unified relationship from the beginning and had made a poor decision for which they were justified in parting ways. *Wow!* I had a hard time concentrating on the rest of the sermon because my brain got hung up on those four little words, *two different worlds colliding*. I know very few relationships that couldn't claim the same thing. And when I got married at age nineteen, I didn't give a whole lot of thought that Dan and I came from totally different worlds. My favorite stories, movies, and songs are about people who come from different worlds and *love* happily ever after.

Dan was raised in a somber, legalistic home. His father was a Conservative Mennonite pastor of a very small congregation in rural Ohio; his mother a quietly submissive homemaker. There were no outward manifestations of romance or joy in their marriage. In fact, the opposite was true. His parents barely tolerated one another most of the sixty-plus years of their marriage and his mother would often leave and come live with us for weeks at a time.

My upbringing was consumed by a desire to please my mother at all costs. As you read in the two versions of my story, there were no male figures in my home or in the extended family. My mother, thrice divorced (she remarried my father briefly), hated men and barely tolerated my dating. I became more like a surrogate spouse for her and when I met Dan at age seventeen, he became a threat because she feared he was going to take me away from her. He also stood up to her in defending me and protecting me from her tirades, which only escalated her intolerance of him.

Once my mother got her degree, she became a much respected high school teacher. Her students loved her and she put most of her energy into the classroom, whether it was earning another degree or teaching others. I was very sheltered, did most of the cleaning and cooking in our home and most of what I learned about life, love, and sex was through my husband after we were married. I was totally unchurched and had never even heard of Mennonites. I loved to dance, wear makeup, and in the '60's I dressed in mini-skirts and lots of jewelry. I was raised on TV, Elvis Presley, and James Bond movies, and rather than having healthy farm-grown food as did Dan, my mother thought Little Debbie snack cakes were one of the major food groups! Dan and I were definitely *two worlds colliding* in every sense. The fact that we were both still teenagers when we married would seem to be another strike against us. Or was it?

We grew up together. We may not have spent our childhoods in the same world, but we definitely learned a lot from what each of us brought to the marriage table. We matured into very different people from those teen years when we were searching for our own identities. Our worlds didn't *collide*. To do so would have meant we were intent upon maintaining self-centered behavior and not encouraging each other to grow and change and become better people. I think our worlds *meshed*.

By definition, mesh means to "fit together harmoniously." By contrast, when one collides, he/she "comes together with violent or direct impact". Dan and I may have been from different worlds, but we each brought from our experience parts we could put together to create *our own NEW world*. We decided quickly to create our own "Haven of Peace." It was our goal from the beginning to change our paradigm and learn to live as new creations. Not only in Christ but within our own marriage and family and home.

Many divorces are granted on the grounds of irreconcilable differences. Often that means, "We are two people who cannot refrain from our own self-centeredness. My needs and desires are more important to me than yours." No marriage is perfect and no one lives *happily ever after* without having their share of conflict, anger, and frustrations. However, agreeing to do what it takes to work out those differences and live harmoniously together is what makes for long-term marriages.

[**Let me insert a caveat here:** I am aware there are abusive relationships that need to be dissolved. I do not believe that once married, one is bound by those vows regardless of how they are treated. I do, however, believe there is a large percentage of marriages that end in divorce because of self-centered expectations and behaviors. A good and successful marriage requires a determination to serve one another in a way that fosters love and kindness. And that takes intentional devotion to working on that relationship **every single day**.]

We are not the same people we were in our teens. Far from it. We are much better, much more secure in who we are and, much happier. And we are still in love. We have *meshed* well for a lifetime; we have learned to love one another and embrace each other's differences and we are determined to live *happily ever after…*

Love the One You're With

Can you remember the moment you fell in love? That pivotal moment when, suddenly, the world stood still. You imagined a full orchestra playing a crescendo of romantic music in the background. Your heart did a flip-flop like you had just dropped over the crest of a gigantic hill on a roller-coaster? That kind of love? Can you remember it?

Our wedding day, March 23, 1968.

I graduated from high school at seventeen and my main interest at that time in my life was boys. I really had no interest in furthering my education. In fact, like many seventeen-year-olds, I hadn't given much thought at all to what I wanted to be when I grew up. But my mother had gotten her life turned around and off welfare by going to college while being a single parent of three little girls so she was adamant that I should attend the local campus in the fall. Part of her argument was, *"If you don't go for any other reason than to meet a good man, it is a good place to start!"* (This coming from a woman who had a chronic and deep disdain for men!) Now, *that* got my attention!

A mutual friend introduced Dan to me *on my very first day* at the Ohio State University branch campus. I was a seventeen-year-old sheltered and very naive freshman and he was a Conservative Mennonite eighteen-year-old sophomore. I needed a ride to campus several days a week and he was ready to jump at the opportunity. We quickly became great friends. But I remember one day as clear as a bell. The day *IT* happened. He had picked me up in his little Renault Dauphine (look it up!) four-speed on the floor. We were talking animatedly when he reached up to adjust the volume on the radio. Instead of bringing his hand back down to rest on the gearshift, he rested it on my knee. Now, come on, you know that feeling. Like an electrical spark happens and you suddenly realize this isn't just a friendship anymore. And that is exactly what happened. In less than a year, we were married. That incident happened in 1967—some years ago. But to this day, I love it when Dan puts his hand on my knee, or pulls me in a bear-hug or snuggles up to keep me warm.

Decades of marriage bring on differing manifestations of love. They may not include all the tingles and butterflies and crescendos of orchestral music, but I challenge you to never forget why you fell in love with the one you love. Because, chances are, the very reasons you did are often the very attributes that cause you to bristle and pull your hair out in frustration. Funny how that happens.

As a very naive seventeen-year-old who never experienced having a father or brother, I cherished the strength and determination I saw in Dan. I still do. I loved his brain and his ability to be decisive and carry through. I still do. And sometimes those very things I most love about him are what drive me mad. Sometimes I have to remind myself that I too have a voice in what happens in our relationship because if I don't, I can quickly become consumed by his more overpowering personality.

Ever have this kind of conversation?

> **Dan:** "Where would you like to go to eat?"
>
> **Joanne:** "I don't know. I'm open to whatever."
>
> **Dan:** "Ok then, let's go to Garcia's."
>
> **Joanne:** "No, I don't want Mexican!"
>
> **Dan:** "Well, how about sushi?"
>
> **Joanne:** "No, I eat there every week with the girls and I'm getting tired of sushi!"
>
> **Dan:** "Why don't you tell me where you would like to go then?!"
>
> **Joanne:** "I said I was open … just not those places."

By now Dan is feeling like Charlie Brown when Lucy has once again retracted the football as he was running to kick it. And I wish I could be more decisive and make the choice without this kind of scenario. But we are different and, after all these decades, we recognize those differences. They don't bother us as much as they did when we were early in our relationship trying to figure each other out.

Every now and then, I think on why I married my dear husband. And I keep a couple of photographs on display in our home of when we were first married and had stars in our eyes and so much love in our hearts we were full to bursting. Our love hasn't diminished, but it certainly has changed. It has grown so much stronger through the years because we have learned to live with each other *in the everyday.* Not just the date nights when everything is perfect, the candles are burning, the orchestra is playing in our heads, and we see nothing but the best in one another. We have been together through some very rough times and clung together in tears and in loss.

How has your love changed for your partner? I challenge you to spend an evening together reminiscing about the first time you knew for certain he/she was *the* one. The *only* one. Perhaps you will hear music you had forgotten was there all the time.

Many marriages would be better if the husband and wife clearly understood that they're on the same side.

—Zig Ziglar

Chapter Two
Family: You Gotta Love 'Em!

> Your success as a family ... our success as a society ... depends not on what happens in the White House, but on what happens inside your house.
>
> —**Barbara Bush (reported in** *The Washington Post*, **June 2, 1990)**

What does your spouse do that really bugs you? Seriously. What annoys you to the point of anger every time it happens? Trust me, if it isn't dealt with, that molehill will grow into a mountain at the most inopportune time. The best time to deal with an irritation is *before* it erupts into a volcanic rage of harsh words and hurt feelings.

When we were married only a few months, I got tired of cleaning the mold off the shower curtain in our tiny trailer bathroom. I calmly asked Dan to pull the curtain open wide after he showered so the mold would not be an issue. I didn't accuse him of making the problem. I didn't say it in anger. I simply asked him to do this as a courtesy to me. And, I never had to ask him again ... ever. In over forty decades. (Why would he not want to please me?)

Does your spouse leave the toilet seat up and it annoys the heck out of you? Not only is it bad Feng Shui (so I have been told), but if your hairbrush accidentally flies out of your hand, Murphy's Law will always land it into the toilet bowl. I like to have the toilet seat and lid closed. Dan doesn't find that worth arguing about.

Pick your battles. Oh, you will have them. But, for Heaven's sake, make them worth the tears and make up *activities!* I used to manicure my nails while watching TV in the evening. Dan cringed if I let nail clippings fall on the floor. So I now get my nails done in a salon. A good compromise, don't you think? Seriously, it was a lot of years that I did my own nails and, out of respect for Dan, I spread a towel over my lap to catch the debris. It was a simple thing really, but listening to what annoys your partner is crucial to having a resentful-free home. Do not misunderstand this admonishment to mean you should not be authentic. But, if you think having the Popeye mentality of *I am what I am!* excuses you from being considerate of others ... especially your spouse ... you had better reconsider marriage.

Marriage is comprised of mutual compromises lovingly centered around a goal of harmony and peace in the home.

What's Your Style?

Personality style plays a huge part in any relationship. If you are familiar with the **DISC** personality profile, you will know the four quadrants:

D=Dominant (task-oriented)
I=Influencing (people-oriented)
S=Steadiness (people-oriented)
C=Compliant (task-oriented)

To paint a picture of these personalities, think of each style as an animal, bird, or car:

D=Lion, Eagle, Ferrari (with lots of power and flash)
I=Otter, Peacock, Mercedes (the more tricked out, the better)
S=Golden Retriever, Dove, Honda Odyssey Minivan (efficient, practical)
C=Beaver, Owl, Volvo Station Wagon (sturdy, safe, and well-crafted)

After reading that list, you probably have a good idea of where you fall, even if you weren't familiar with the profile. And you can probably easily determine who, in that grouping, might be the likely leader. If you are married to a High D personality, you probably don't need anyone to tell you who's in charge! Most people have a little of all the components in them, but usually two are most prominent and tend to be the primary components of one's personality.

Dan and I began using personality profiles in helping others and to better understand ourselves about twenty-five years ago. If you think they are a hoax or not reliable, I encourage you to take one yourself. If you are honest in answering the brief **DISC** profile, you will be amazed at the percentage of information you get back that rings true about you. Yes, you can skew the test. You can try to be something contrary to your nature, but what's the point? And, interestingly, the test usually catches on to the inconsistencies and points it out to you. (If you would like to take a computerized **DISC** profile, go to www.48Days.com/store/personality-profiles. You will get a lengthy report that will amaze you!)

Without getting too technical about the profile, let me emphasize that a grasp of our own *and* each other's personality has helped our marriage exponentially. And it has helped us better understand our children, friends, and employees. Dan is a high **D-C**. I am a high **S-I**. We are total opposites. If we were a young couple looking to get married, we would have many well-meaning people tell us we would be high risk. Too late for that. We didn't know any better back in 1968!

Actually, I like to think our personalities fit together like a hand in a glove. One needs the other to be complete. I know you are thinking about the famous line from Jerry McGuire, "You complete me!" And as sappy as that may seem to some, I do think opposites attract. And they can also destroy. Be careful how you use your innate style in a relationship. It can make your marriage an amazing adventure or it can break it into a million miserable pieces. Here's a sentence you should never forget: Any strength can become a weakness if overused!

Our strengths can turn against us if we aren't aware of how they can be our downfall. Being aware is the key to managing well our God-given resources. Here are examples of how your style can be either a strength or a weakness:

D= Confident and direct, bold and determined OR hurts other's feelings, overlooks details.

I= Outgoing, good talker, creative, and energetic OR wastes time, won't be quiet and listen.

S= Steady, loyal, patient, and reliable OR slow to act, unrealistic, stays in the background.

C= Loves detail, factual, logical, and predictable OR can appear rigid, serious, and resistant to change.

Knowing my own personality and my tendency towards verbosity … (Why say anything in a sentence when you can use a paragraph?) … makes me more aware of how to talk to and listen to others. I know Dan wants just the facts and the bottom line. I know I love to tell a story when relating information. But paring down to the Cliff Notes for Dan when he is in *task mode* makes him seem less a jerk and helps me not get my feelings hurt.

Any strength can become a weakness if overused!

Knowing Dan's tendency to be the visionary and the dreamer with new ideas popping up daily has been an interesting adventure for me with my **S** personality. I could have easily lived in the same house forever … married to a guy who worked nine to five and retired after thirty years. Being married to a high-**D** personality has stretched me … sometimes more than I wanted to be stretched. But it works both ways. Dan has become much more aware of how to deal with his family members and his clients because he knows he can have a tendency to be overbearing, offensive, and too direct. Understanding personality styles helps you relate better to everyone, especially in your own home.

Once, Ashley, the baby of the family and the only girl (who could wrap her father around her little finger), studied her Dad's profile to be able to adequately give a case for her having a puppy. She was about thirteen years old and wanted to present a proposal to her Daddy to rescue a dog from the local pound. She wrote it all out (while perusing his profile) in a way that would seem appropriate for him to accept as well thought-out. And well-thought out it was indeed. She got her puppy.

Each of our adult children will tell you we required anyone they seriously dated fill out a **DISC** profile. Nathan, our son-in-law, very humorously relates how, after several dates with Ashley, he was presented with a test to fill out to see if he was accepted as a suitable candidate for courting our daughter. Said it scared him silly. But filling out that profile confirmed to us he would make a great match for our strong-willed High-**D** daughter. Each of them has embraced the strengths of the other and their happy marriage is proof.

Who's in Control?

Understanding your personality and that of your spouse is the first step to keeping peace in your home. Usually someone takes the lead, but control is another matter. Dan is a born leader. No doubt about it. I can lead when no one else will, but will gladly acquiesce to someone who will take charge. We know that about each other. The key to peace in our home has been to be respectful of the other person, be it spouse or child. I can get my feelings hurt if I am treated harshly and talked down to. I have about zero **D** in my personality by nature but to survive in a family of high-**D**s, I have learned to speak out, be more decisive, and stick up for myself. Not a bad trade off. We can learn from one another. Dan has learned to listen to and even appreciate my lengthy stories of events and adventures. He knows I have a lot of words in me and he knows my overly compassionate heart. He respects and admires that in me. We temper one another. I like to think we round out the edges.

When it comes to parenting, we have always covered each other's back. We have agreed on a family mission statement, have a firm value system by which we parent, and we support one another in how that is carried out. Undermining one another's efforts would be counter-productive and destructive. And there is one important point we both firmly agree on that we feel undermines many marriages: A peaceful and loving home is not controlled by the children!

Children learn respect by watching their parents interact with one another and others outside the home. They need to respect that Mommy and Daddy need time to talk without interruption and need time to themselves to function well as a family unit. I once read that a parent who refuses to discipline their child does so because they lack self-confidence. That parent is afraid his/her child will no longer love them. That was an insight that stuck with me all the years of setting boundaries and guidelines for our children.

> The best way to raise positive children in a
> negative world is to have parents who love them
> unconditionally and serve as excellent role models.
> —**Zig Ziglar**

In his best-selling book, *Raising Positive Kids in a Negative World*, Zig Ziglar quotes Dr. J. Allan Peterson, who says,

> Partnership must precede parenthood. A man is a husband first, father second, businessman third. A woman is a wife first, mother second, career woman third. A strong marriage precedes a strong family. Marriage is permanent; parenthood is temporary. Marriage is central; parenthood is secondary. Marriage is the hub; children are the spokes. The child-centered home is poor training for the child, poor marriage insurance, poor preparation for the empty nest. Your partner is first, before children, job or career. A man must love his wife as himself, and the wife must honor her husband (as stated in Ephesians 5:33).

I have seen many homes where it is evident the children rule. The parents can't talk without continual interruption. The house is chaotic and there are no boundaries. Ironically, the parents are unhappy and the children are usually not happy either. Children crave boundaries and because they are innately eager to please, they are happiest when they know they are making their parents happy. Learning to respect that their parents need a date night, need uninterrupted time to talk, and need some separation from their children is healthy and necessary for a happy home. When the children are in control, they grow up with an inordinate amount of entitlement; they handle disappointment poorly and get easily frustrated when everything doesn't go their way. This is not parenting. This is enabling bad behavior. It is not healthy for a marriage and usually produces self-centered, demanding children that no one enjoys having around.

The best thing you can do for your children is to have a strong marriage. Christian marriage counselors emphasize that child-centered homes inevitably become dysfunctional to some degree. It turns out that the best way to ensure our children are nurtured is to displace them from the center of the family. Counselor after counselor agrees that when the husband and the wife put their children ahead of each other it sucks the vibrancy from their marriage, which harms the kids. The fact is that what kids want is much less important than what married couples need…We need to operate our marriages at an adult level, with husbands and wives in ministry to one another rather than in servanthood to their children (Rev. Donald Sensing, Trinity UMC, Franklin, TN, from a sermon on Marriage and Family, 2002).

Wonder why your whole family doesn't get invited to dinner? Embarrassed at how your child screams and demands and throws temper tantrums in the grocery store? Has it been months (or years) since you felt you could complete an entire sentence or train of thought with your spouse, the neighbor, or your best friend? Who's in control?

> A peaceful and loving home is
> not controlled by the children!

Dan and I wanted to raise children who were liked by others and who got invited to the homes of friends and family. That meant teaching them to be respectful of people and of their personal possessions. In other words, be

"No Boundaries" painting of granddaughter, Saoirse Sky Angaza by Joanne Miller.

polite, be considerate of others talking, don't jump on the furniture, or get into everything. Ask for permission to touch. Simple guidelines that should be incorporated into any family who wants their home to be filled with happiness, love, and peace. This takes time. It takes the confidence to believe your child will love you even when you say no and even when you allow that child to reap the consequences of his/her behavior. Trust me, your child won't be a saint even with discipline. Our three knew where the bathroom was in about every store we shopped regularly and that wasn't because of their need to use the facilities. Often it was because they needed an "attitude adjustment!"

And while we are on this subject, I would suggest one more important rule to healthy child rearing. Don't be the little boy who continually cried wolf. Making idle threats your child has heard so many times and which he knows you won't follow through just exacerbates the problem. "If you do that one more time, we are leaving!" "If you don't stop whining, you are going to take a nap!" Seriously, maybe you *do* need to leave the store or maybe that child really *is* overly tired and needs to take a nap. Take into consideration what is truly going on with the misbehavior and take the proper steps to rectify the situation. If the child continues to misbehave and you follow through on leaving the store (even if it is to drive around the block until he believes you are serious), he will know you mean what you say. You set the guidelines and boundaries and then *be prepared to enforce them.* You will be surprised at how others will welcome your children with open arms!

I don't want my children to fear me,
or feel that I am their master.
I have no desire to control them or for them to fit in.
I only want to inspire them to live as examples of love.
I consider it a great honor to play a role
in their wondrous journey.

—Jared Angaza, from a blog post, May 21, 2015,
titled *These Divine, Limitless Souls Are Not Our Own*

Mind Your Manners

We went to lunch at a local restaurant, played a favorite card game while we waited for our food, then came home to take our usual Sunday Sabbath respite (nap). As we got out of the car, I thanked Dan for taking me to lunch. I have been thanking him for decades. I will keep thanking him for … um … a lot more decades!

The women's liberation movement of the 1960s and '70s resulted in a lot of positive change for women's rights, but also left in its wake confusion as to how men should treat women. I find this exceedingly unfortunate. I have witnessed women be enraged because a man would actually open the door for them. After all, just because they are female doesn't leave them incapable of the strength to open their own door. No wonder men were often left speechless and in a quandary about how to be gentlemen. The gender role lines have been greatly blurred through the years. I am just traditional enough in my thinking to blame this phenomenon on the demise of common courtesy among the sexes.

It is so important to teach children *how* to be considerate and mannerly. We felt it important that our children understand the difference between indoor manners, outdoor behavior, and in public respect and consideration. When they were teens, I took the boys separately on dates to teach them how to be mannerly and respect a lady. Dan took Ashley out, so she would know how to set a standard for how she should be treated by a mate. My children had high expectations for spouses. Kindness and consideration were high priorities. Our sons were in high regard for dating. The girls they dated always told us they loved how they were treated.

It Is Important to *Him* if It Is Important to *Me*

> Serving each other is never a burden
> when done out of love.

After four decades, Dan still thanks me when I make his favorite muffins he likes every morning for breakfast. He knows it is time-consuming to make them and he respects the time I take for him. When I bring something to his attention that needs to be repaired, disposed of, or moved, I rarely have to ask twice. *It is important to him if it is important to me.* Nagging isn't necessary if we are really listening to what is being asked and our desire is to please the other.

Recently on a rainy day, I felt like a good cup of hot tea was in order. I didn't go in and make myself a cup of tea without asking Dan if he also wanted a cup. If we are watching a good movie in the evening and Dan goes into the kitchen to get a snack, he will ask me if I would like something. And he will gladly bring it to me if I do.

Demanding to be waited on is *not* love and a desire to serve, but rather self-absorption and a need for control. That kind of behavior causes resentment and anger. Somewhere down the line, the perpetrator of that abuse will break down any relationship, whether it be between couples or between parent and child.

It never occurred to me in 70 years that
kindness was important in a relationship.
Fascination, sex appeal, intelligence, yes.
Why aren't we taught that kindness matters?

—**Jane Fonda in an interview in AARP magazine (June/July 2015)**

All I'm Asking Is for a Little R-E-S-P-E-C-T

I am often asked what one piece of advice I have for young couples who want to create a Haven of Peace and build a great relationship. Without question or hesitation, I would say a one-word answer … *Respect!* It pains me greatly to see how badly people treat those they love the most, especially when it concerns spousal and parent/child relationships. We are asked how we garnered respect from our children; and how have we maintained a stable, uncomplicated, and loving relationship over the years. It is that simple R-E-S-P-E-C-T that Aretha Franklin belted out decades ago. *All we need is a little respect!* No, actually we need a LOT of respect. And simple, old-fashioned manners. And courtesies. Where did they go? Remember the days when Miss Manners was a popular newspaper column? How about Emily Post? Teaching manners and respect *used* to be so popular, we actually sent our children to classes to learn how to be polite in society. Now we send our kids to martial arts to learn how to annihilate others.

Somewhere along the way, we have lost our sense of propriety. We have shelved traditional manners and formalities and replaced them with sloppiness, casualness, and even disdain. Just because we can. In searching for our own authenticity, we have decided that being authentic is tantamount to such an acceptance of informality that we have forgotten how to be courteous and respectful. Come as you are has gone to the extreme, and most formalities in daily life have been replaced by total nonchalance.

You can't get respect if you don't give respect.

Respect is often most violated in the home, and therefore not practiced outside the home in public. I have actually heard people say they want to be able to be themselves at home and not to put on any pretenses. Seriously? If I understand this correctly, this is the message: "I'm going to be an inconsiderate jerk at home, so get used to it!" The irony here is those very people often demand their children say "please" and "thank you" and treat others, *not* as they see in their own home, but as they are *told* to do or to risk dire consequences.

If children see good manners and polite consideration between their parents and from parents to children, they generally treat others in the same way. Seldom do you see children who come from respectful and loving homes turn into bullies, tyrants or abusive adults.

Respect is taught at home. Here are some ways you can exhibit and promote respect in your home to make it more peaceful and harmonious:

- Teach your children to be observant of their surroundings and, if someone is talking, to wait their turn. I have observed our daughter and son-in-law teaching their young daughters to wait to get their attention if they want to speak. I have heard them repeatedly tell their children, "Listen to what is going on and who is talking instead of interrupting." So now I see their children come into a room and just lay a hand on their parent's arm to indicate, "I want to say something" or "I need your attention." They are teaching respect from an early age and it is quite admirable.
- If a door is closed, it usually means privacy is preferred. Never just barge in and expect to be welcomed without resentment. Even young children need privacy and quiet time. If you respect their privacy, they will learn to respect yours.

- Teach good manners at the table. Eating can be rigid and formal with little interaction (as it usually was at Dan's family's table growing up) or it can be full of fighting, bickering, and arguing (as it was for me growing up). Dan and I chose to have mealtime be a time of laughter, for sharing our day and practicing good manners. If children don't learn at home, they likely won't learn anywhere else. Seems there is a dearth of etiquette classes these days.

- If you begin taking time for developing your own relationship as a couple when the children are young, they will learn to respect you for it ... and It will spill over into their own marriages. Putting the children to bed early won't hurt them, and it will give you a couple hours in the evening to relax together, sip a glass of wine, and talk without interruption. As the children get older, require they spend time in their rooms before bed just quieting down and allowing you time alone.

- Always be honest. Never condone lying or cheating. Just the slightest bent in the wrong direction tells a child or a spouse that you can't be trusted. I think each of our children can remember a specific instance when they were punished for lying, and it made an indelible memory they never wanted to repeat.

- Never allow back talk. Children who don't hear their parents be disrespectful to one another rarely express themselves disrespectfully once they realize the consequences. Often it can be stopped by helping the child understand how hurtful that behavior can be. Most children have a strong desire to please. If you get angry and yell or accuse, you will likely see that same behavior in your children and certainly you will receive it from your spouse.

Here's a Step in the *Write* Direction!

How often do you get a hand-written thank you for all the hard work you put into deciding on, buying, wrapping, and giving a gift that you hope the recipient enjoys? How do you know that it was the right gift? Did it fit? Was it appreciated? How do you know if you don't hear a word about it? It is a pet peeve of mine.

I once had someone tell me when I was spouting off about my dismay on this very subject, that it is easy for me to send cards and notes to others because it was my gifting. *Really?* So does that mean that only polite, well-mannered people are expected to send appreciation and treat others respectfully and anyone else is exempt? *If that isn't your gifting, you are **off the hook?*** I was dumbfounded by that cop-out and still am. Using one of Dr. Phil's favorite lines, I would like to ask, "How's that working for you?"

You reap what you sow. Not only is it a Biblical principle but it is a LIFE principle that works. I know you can teach your children well and still have problems with them. Certainly we have had our share. But I know we worked hard to set a good example and that is the undergirding of our own successful relationships.

Something to think about:

How are you treating your spouse?

What do your children see in the way you communicate with one another?

Who are they emulating?

What are they watching on TV and in the movies that influence their behavior?

What are they repeatedly allowed to get by with that is creating bad habits?

Do Unto Others

The Golden Rule is taught to kids in churches, schools, and in homes across the world. Matthew 7:12 holds the key to happy relationships and a happy life. Treat others like you want them to treat you. *It ain't complicated!* Trust me, if you yell, demand, or nag, you will likely not gain respect from anyone. Don't expect it.

I love that Dan still opens a door and waits for me to go first. I love that he offers to carry my packages. How stupid would it be for me to tell him I can do it myself (which I certainly can) and act offended? I also love that Dan doesn't complain when I ruin his new black shirt by accidentally getting bleach on it in the laundry. Accidents happen. We both know that. I didn't set out to deliberately ruin a good shirt.

Case in point:
One day, years ago, I had had a full day of motherhood. Kevin was eight years old and Jared was an infant. I had invited a friend of Kevin's over to play, and they had been pretty rowdy that day. I was eager to return the visiting child to his parents, so when Dan arrived home from his work at the car lot, I asked him to watch the baby while I took the little boy home. I kissed Dan goodbye, grabbed the car keys, ushered the boys into the back seat, started the engine, put the car in gear, and backed right into the car Dan had just parked behind me in the driveway. A car that was not his, but one he had driven home from the car lot. I couldn't believe I actually did that. *Stop laughing!* I was mortified. It was a big car. Why didn't I see it? I got out and assessed the damage. It wasn't a pretty sight. My rear bumper had made a huge indentation on the front grill of the other car. Of course, the boys in the back seat were staring bug-eyed wondering if I had lost my mind. I was wondering myself!

I went inside the house to tell Dan. He, of course, had heard the crunch of metal against metal and knew exactly what I had done. Before I tried to defend myself or apologize, he put his arms around me and said, "Honey, I think you have had a bad day." That was all. No yelling, telling me how stupid I was. He just calmly walked outside and backed the damaged vehicle out of my way.

Of course, I apologized and felt awful that I had done something so ridiculous, but he just shrugged it off. Realistically, it wasn't possible to reverse what happened, so why get bent out of shape? He knew that. And he knew I would never have done something like that on purpose. Accidents happen. And that is a fact. I asked him recently if they sold the car with the wrinkled front grill or if he got it repaired. He couldn't even remember. Sometimes a little perspective is all that is needed in a situation.

Something to think about:
How would you react if your spouse had done something so crazy, especially if you think it might cost you money for repairs? How would you want to be treated if you had been the one who had caused the accident?

Another case in point:
I had a friend visiting from out of town. I drove us both to a local restaurant for lunch in my cute red Volvo Turbo. We had a great lunch and then returned to the car. I turned the key and nothing. No sound at all. Now, I know cars pretty well. I knew it wasn't a battery issue because it would have given a little sound. I tried several times and the car simply would not make a sound.

It was a hot summer day and I knew our son, Jared, was at our house doing some painting, so I called him, got him off a ladder, and told him my predicament. He immediately said, "I'll be there in a few minutes. No worries." Jared drove all the way across town and when he arrived, he took the key and tried to start the Volvo. Nothing. He reached down and put the car in Park, turned the key, and it started right up. *I was mortified.* I know cars better than most men, and I had tried to start it without checking to see what GEAR it was in? *Had I lost my mind?* I was so embarrassed and felt bad that I had interrupted Jared's work to come and do something so simple that I should have seen myself. I apologized profusely! He hugged me and said, "No worries, Mom! Welcome to MY world! I needed a break anyway!" And that was it. He never told me how foolish I was or got impatient or angry because I screwed up. Nope. He had been in too many situations where he had messed up himself. And he had been taught to respect and honor other people, not to tear them down or make them feel stupid.

These events stand out in my mind because I know how blessed I am to have a family who treats each other with respect and good manners. It isn't an act or manipulation on their part. *It is innate in their character because it was taught early on.* Our children had seen their parents treat each other with respect and with politeness. Children learn the most from watching their parents. If Dan had yelled at me for being stupid years ago, Jared would have undoubtedly yelled at me for being stupid years later.

Author and motivational speaker (and a long-time family hero) Zig Ziglar had his own version of the Golden Rule. He would say, over and over, "You can have everything in life you want if you help enough other people get what they want." A wise man, indeed. I feel sure he would attribute his happy sixty-six-year marriage (he died in 2012) to his belief in and application of the Golden Rule.

Something to think about:
What are you teaching your children by your example?

What example of love and service are you modeling for them?

Learning How to Fight

When I was growing up, I lived in a home where fighting was common. Yelling, screaming, cursing, and arguing, hitting, and pulling hair was a part of my life. No wonder I wanted desperately to change my branch of the family tree. Dan's way of getting through difficult times was to walk away. Ignore it. Pretend it didn't exist. Obviously both of us had a lot to learn about "fighting" in our marriage.

I cringe at using the word *fighting*. The definition of that word is to overpower or to fiercely counteract. Another is to have physical conflict. Neither Dan nor I have ever felt it was necessary to fight. If true fighting is a part of your relationship, stop reading this book and find a good counselor quickly! There are better ways to conflict resolution than getting physical, loud, or abusive.

Admittedly, Dan and I have had our differences of opinion and our conflicts. I don't want to give the impression we have never had any arguments. But to say we have fought is simply way too harsh. We have never raised a hand toward one another. I have never heard Dan raise his voice to me or to the children. I will admit there were a few times when my voice might have raised a few decibels above the norm. But fight? Come on. That happens on TV and in the movies. People act crazy, scream, and curse at each other and call each other vile names.

I know from my own background that families can act like they hate each other and some do physical and emotional harm. It saddens me to hear other couples talk about the horrible fights they have and what they say to each other. Words leave scars. I know. If violent conflicts happen in your home, you had better prepare yourself for raising children who also abuse. They often become school bullies and are usually very poor spouse material. And, please, if you are a victim of physical abuse, get help. For yourself and for your children. Physical abuse should never be tolerated in any relationship.

Dealing with Conflict

Dan used to walk away from conflict. Just shut down. His avoidance and lack of resolution to a problem within our relationship would really upset me. And because I was such a "stuffer" with my feelings (due to very dire consequences growing up if I spoke my mind), we often glossed over conflict till it resolved itself in some form or till one of us acquiesced. But I remember a time when I had had enough of that kind of behavior …

Dan had come home during the day, and I had some urgent and disturbing issues I needed to discuss with him. We were in his little office in our home, and he was standing near his desk. In the middle of my unleashing some pent-up frustration, I noticed he had his hand on the telephone on his desk, obviously waiting for me to finish so he could get back to his work. What his posture was telling me was, "Hurry up with this prattle. I have more important things to attend to." I calmly walked over and physically took his hand off the phone, looked him in the eyes, and said firmly, "Listen to me. I need you to hear me out and not dismiss what I have to say as unimportant." I then walked over to his office door and closed it so he couldn't walk away. We continued the conversation. Needless to say, I made my point and he listened. It was a turning point in our communication.

Long ago I learned a sales principle from Dan that we have always tried to incorporate into our family dynamics. The result of any disagreement should end in a "win-win" for each party. Not an "I win-you lose" result. That sometimes means compromising, but no one gets the short end of the stick. In the long run, neither one of us wants to control or dominate so that the other feels fear, disappointment, or condemnation. The ultimate goal is to live in harmony, not in anger or war.

Case in point:

A couple years ago, Dan and I were driving down a road near our home. He remarked about the dark blotch in the road, saying it was a big road kill spot. Somehow I felt certain that dark spot was caused by a car that had caught on fire, so I corrected him. He said he was pretty sure it was road kill and I said again I thought he was wrong. He simply said, "Maybe you're right." and dropped it. I felt smug in my "rightness." But a long time later, I realized Dan *had* been right and I was misinformed. I began to feel bad that I had insisted on his acceptance of my correction and knew he had assumed the position of neutrality instead of making me feel stupid or feeling the need to prove me wrong. I knew in my heart I owed him an apology even though a long time had passed since the initial conversation. It was the right thing to do. So one day while passing by that spot, I told him I needed to apologize and I did. He didn't even remember the incident but thanked me for being considerate. I believe it's that kind of consideration that prevents a lot of arguments for us. It puts a lot of deposits into our relational bank account.

Something to think about:

How do you resolve conflict? Think about this long and hard. Be truthful to yourself.

Can you remember times when you had to prove your point and make sure you won the argument?

Do you ever see yourself in *competition,* rather than in *compatibility,* with one another?

Nice and Simple

My friend, Nick Pavlidis, is a young attorney on the East Coast. He came to one of the 48 Days events at our Sanctuary to learn more about being a coach. What he learned surprised him. He tells the story in his book, *Confessions of a Terrible Husband, Lessons Learned from a Lumpy Couch* (2015, Free Agent Press). He says that, on his way home, his wheels were turning because "what started out as a business became a life lesson (he) couldn't afford to miss." He recounts very candidly how he watched Dan and me work together with respect and love. He witnessed the close bond of our family, and he realized he wanted that more than he wanted the fame, money, and prestige of climbing the corporate ladder.

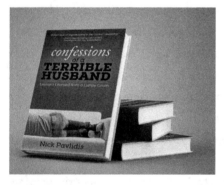

I highly recommend Nick's book for both genders to read. It is highly engaging, humorous, and very real. (Check out his website www. ATerribleHusband.com.) He realizes he is a continual work in progress and underscores the importance of respecting, honoring, and loving your spouse. When he returned home, he began a process that ultimately led him down a totally different life path from what he had planned.

Here are a few excerpts from Nick's journey into understanding the importance of prioritizing his goals:

"For several weeks, I quietly observed the world around me. I looked and I listened. And I asked tough questions of those folks who were viewed as "on the top" of the industry at a number of large law firms in the area. I asked them what it took to make it as far as they had. I asked about their family lives. I asked about where they were at my age, and at my career stage, and what they did to become so successful. A pattern emerged. A scary one. Almost without exception, the "success stories" included passing references to "my ex-wife," "my first wife," or "my ex." Some even included "my second wife."

After a few of these conversations, I'd ask how their careers affected their relationships. Many of their answers sounded like, "Well, I got married too young because my first wife didn't understand that this is what you need to do to be successful in the industry." When I asked about their kids, *it was often a similar response, including* something to the effect of "they know this is what I have to do if they want to have nice things, take nice vacations, or get the latest gadgets."

By this time, it was early 2013. I was in the center of the world, New York City, working in a corner office on the thirty-first floor of a high-rise building overlooking Central Park. To everyone on the outside, I was on top of the world. But now I knew it was not a sustainable arrangement if I wanted to avoid telling stories about my "first wife" to a young lawyer looking to find his or her way twenty years later.

… I needed to shift my mindset to focus on what I could do to be a better husband and father for my family so that when I die, an honest eulogy will include 'a loving husband and father' instead of just "a hardworking lawyer."

… Certainly, stress tends to increase when your circumstances and seasons are such that more unexpected or not-completely-controllable obligations arise. But the way you and your spouse act, talk, support, engage, and otherwise treat each other crosses seasons and circumstances, traveling through time and space."

Nick and Andrea Pavlidis Family.

At the close of his book, Nick tells how he interviewed couples who had been married many decades. He says, "… their advice sounds nice and simple. Who could argue with respect, support, communication, faithfulness, honesty, and truth?"

It really is simple to figure out. It doesn't take a master's degree in communication to intuit that how you treat your spouse, your children, and your friends lays the foundation for future success in just about anything you pursue. What is *not* so simple is implementing those principles; the consideration and selflessness that garner respect, support, and integrity. Like anything worthwhile, there is a lot of work necessary. A good marriage or good parenting doesn't just happen by accident.

Chapter Three

What's Your Mission?

B ack in about 1990, we decided to draw up a family mission statement. Most businesses, schools, and organizations had mission statements. There were many books being published about the importance of writing a *personal* mission statement. Our kids were at that age where they were becoming more independent and headstrong, and we were looking for ways to take us out of the role of "Rule Enforcement Officer." So why not have a *family* mission statement?

I had read a magazine article that included a message I thought embraced what we stood for. We had a family meeting; each of the children and Dan and I agreed it was what we wanted to represent as a family. Because *all family members* had agreed to adopt this philosophy, when someone did something that violated our mission statement, instead of a parent being accusatory or angry, all we needed to ask was, "Was what you did (or said) in line with our family mission statement?" It took us out of the hot seat in being the judge and jury so the kids couldn't blame anyone but themselves for their transgression.

How do you come up with a family mission statement? Just decide what you want your family to represent:

- How do you want to be treated?
- How do you want to treat others?
- What do you want to be of high priority in your home?
- What do you want to be of low priority?
- What kind of atmosphere do you want to achieve?

Talk openly about what disturbs you in the family dynamics and how can you best avoid that behavior. You may run across something in scripture or in a poem or in another mission statement that could be the basis for what you draw up. Or you might create your own from scratch with everyone adding a line or two. Ours came mainly from an article I read in Reader's Digest, so it isn't original, but captured what we wanted to emulate:

A Safe Place

In a safe place, people are kind.
Sarcasm, fighting, back-biting and name-calling are exceptions.
Kindness, consideration, and forgiveness are the way of life.
In a safe place, there is laughter.
Not just the canned laughter of television,
but *real* laughter that comes from sharing meaningful work and play.
In a safe place, there are rules.
The rules are few and fair
and are made by the people who live and work there,
including the children.
In a safe place, people listen to one another.
They care about one another and show that they do.
Please God, make this *a safe place.*

(Excerpt from *Not Like the Other Kids*, condensed from *Turnabout Children by Mary MacCracken* as published in *Reader's Digest*, March 1990)

I suggest you call everyone together for a family meeting. We used to have them at least once a month. Make it sound like a lot of fun. Start off with a great dinner together (require everyone's presence), maybe play a game to set the mood, and then have a talk. For us, family nights included a time to talk about grievances, frustrations, disappointments, accomplishments, desires, family vacations, schedules, rules, expectations, etc. If a family meeting started to veer into a gripe fest, it was quickly rechanneled into a more positive direction. Sometimes these meetings were serious and covered some important issues, and sometimes they were just crazy fun. But it was definitely a time to communicate freely without fear of condemnation or judgment. It was our SAFE PLACE. We always wanted the children to feel they could be totally honest and open about their feelings.

During a family meeting, you can ask each child to submit his/her ideas for consideration in adopting a mission statement. It doesn't matter how long or involved it is. The important issue is you all agree with it wholeheartedly. That way, if it is violated (and it will be), the parent or child will know he/she is wrong and has no one to blame but themselves. If your children are very young, make your mission statement very basic and short. It can be revised as the seasons of child-rearing change.

Let me give you another hint on how to make this work well in your home. Don't laugh. Write or print out the Statement and tape it next to the toilet in every bathroom of the house. Seriously. It really works. Kids memorize easily and, if something is right there where they can see it many times during the day for days on end, they *will* memorize it. Stick it on mirrors, the refrigerator ... whatever works ... but know that it is important everyone sees it often and it becomes ingrained in their minds, so when someone is abusing the rules, they know immediately they are guilty. And don't be at all surprised if your five-year-old brings it to your attention if you have let something slip that violates what she has memorized!

Creating Memories and Celebrations

Dan and grandson Caleb playing Connect Four.

A peaceful home should be full of fun and laughter. A somber home is usually not one that elicits fond memories. I can't think of a better way to create amazing memories within families than to regularly play games. We started as soon as the kids were old enough to understand how to play *Candyland, The Memory Game* and *Chutes and Ladders*. Even now we are always on a quest to find new and interesting games we can play with friends and family and with just the two of us.

I had a conversation with my grandson, Caleb, who had just moved into his dorm room for his first year at college. Caleb and I have been playing word games on our electronic devices now for at least a year. *WordFeud* and *UpWords* are our favorites. He is quite good. His vocabulary has grown to include words most people have never heard of or would use in a lifetime. And he beats me. Often. And every single day, playing these games with him helps me stay in touch with that sweet boy. We chat through the game and sometimes we even do FaceTime while we are playing, so we talk and play at the same time. We feel connected and close even though we are a thousand miles apart.

Caleb told me he had spent a couple of days at home playing games and having fun with his family (he has six siblings) before he went off to college. Then he excitedly told me he had convinced his parents to get the apps and play word games with him on their iPhones so they could continue the fun when he moved out—a great way to stay connected in a way that is a continuation of fun they have shared through his years living at home.

What your child most wants—and needs—is to be with you with no goal in mind beyond the joy of spending time together. He wants you to take pleasure in him, play with him, and listen to him. Nothing bolsters his self-esteem more! So why not pull out an old board game or a deck of cards tonight? Playing games is an easy and excellent way to spend unhurried, enjoyable time together.

We have some great photos of family gatherings around game nights. We have laughed till we cried. Many times. Serious fun. Dan and I have a hard time understanding when someone says they don't play games. They don't know how. Did they never get down on the floor with a six-year-old and watch the glee on her face when she matched the two clown faces in *Memory* and got an extra turn? Did they miss the fun with a teenager as he bought up Park Place and Boardwalk (*Monopoly*) and raked in the rent fees? Did they never sit down with a group of family and friends and play the *Dictionary Game* or *Catch Phrase*? I can't imagine all the fun we would have missed in our family if it weren't for game nights.

When our children were in their early years of middle school, we started having Family Night once a week. We began with a great dinner, usually a family favorite using the nice china (it looked expensive, but it came from a garage sale), cloth napkins, and candles on the table. We discussed issues, experiences, and plans over dinner in a pleasant manner while eating our meal.

Our oldest son, Kevin, and family playing Scrabble.

Then we quickly cleaned up and started the games. We played until bedtime when we were all exhausted from laughter and delight.

Interestingly, it wasn't long before the children wanted to invite their friends and our Family Nights expanded to Family and Friends Nights. For many of our children's friends, it was the highlight of their week. Now those friends are raising children of their own and have remarked to us how meaningful those times with our family were for them. It meant a lot to them to be included as family and to see what fun we had together.

Dan's family home was a somber and quiet place. No cards or loud games were allowed. I often visited my cousin, Judy Lynn, who was only three months older than I. We played Canasta and other games till the wee hours, laughing and enjoying girl-talk. When I got to college, I would often spend hours in the cafeteria playing card games with friends. So when Dan came into my life, I taught him how to play. We used to be addicted to *Gin Rummy* and kept a running score for years. We even played it on our honeymoon!

Today, we get together with friends for game nights, playing *Euchre, Tourney Whist, Catch Phrase, Farkle,* and others. When the kids come to visit, we all gather round the dining room table to play, laugh, and reminisce—the very table that stood in the Miller family dining room when Dan was young. We inherited it from his parents. I've written about all the games and conversations that we played around that table. When Dan and I began to have children, we brought the laughter of game-playing into the Miller family. So many great memories.

When Dan and I are waiting at a restaurant or airport, we pull out our deck of cards and play a round or two. Yes, we have actually missed a flight because we were engrossed in our game. We carry a deck of *Quiddler* cards in each of our cars, and I carry a deck of regular playing cards in my purse all the time. We are known at many restaurants as "the couple who plays cards".

Games offer a great opportunity for children to learn better social skills and how to process winning and losing. Games teach how to think spatially, outside the box. They teach colors, numbers, sequences, memory, facts, finances, history, and life skills. Games teach communication, how to wait, share, and take turns—even how to resolve arguments congenially. Games teach how to problem-solve and that is something we all need.

If you missed playing games as a child, you won't be sorry if you start with your own children. If you are past that, it isn't too late to start making game nights a part of your family memories. You will find amazing bonding opportunities in those moments.

Dan and I will probably play cards in the old folks' home and laugh our way into the Pearly Gates. I hope we will see you there with game boards in hand.

The Oak Table

In Loving Memory of Rev. Ray F. Miller and Clara Rosa Miller
Written in 2001

I find myself smiling as I reverently stroke the grain of the old oak table with a soft cloth and fragrant lemon oil. Both the table and the fragrance evoke precious memories.

I have recently acquired the oak dining table and chairs from my husband's parent's home. The set was in continual use as my husband grew from childhood into grandfather-hood.

In 1966, I was privileged to be introduced to that grand table as I ate my first meal with the family who would soon welcome me into their own. In 1970, the first grandchild, our first son, joined us as he graduated from high-chair to the special "child's chair" that elevated him to the right height to enjoy his meals with the grown-ups. Many grandchildren have followed. In 1995, the first great-grandchild, our grandson, joined in the laughter and the memories around the huge oak centerpiece.

My parents-in-law have moved into a lovely retirement home. One day, a few months ago, they asked me what I would like from their large family estate of many years. There was no hesitation on my part. In fact, I was sitting at that old oak table when asked the question. I immediately spread my

Ray and Clara Miller wedding day.

hands and arms along the grain of that table and said "This table and these chairs." I further told them, around the lump in my throat, that I have so very many fond memories of wonderful meals, laughter, talk, bantering, and game-playing while gathered around that table. I told them I wanted to be the one to pass on those memories, through that table, to my own children and grandchildren.

It is a pretty piece of furniture and very sturdy. Takes two men and a policeman to move it. But its looks are inconsequential. The tales it could tell if brought to life are what I truly care about.

I know I am an incurable romantic. I make no apologies for that. It is easy for me to remember the good things and not dwell on those things which are troublesome. It is my nature and my choice. I remember beginning a tradition around that table of placing random questions on slips of paper in a dish which we passed around at major mealtimes such as Easter or Thanksgiving or Christmas. Each individual—including the children—chose a slip of paper from the dish, read it, and thought about their response while eating the meal. After eating, each person would read his or her question and respond aloud. It was not unusual to see the glisten of tears in an eye or hear a cacophony of laughter at the responses. It was during one of these times that we all sat spellbound while Grandpa told us how he met, courted, and proposed to Grandma. No one had heard that story before ... a precious memory.

I remember many bowls of popcorn being passed around. I remember home-made pies eaten with scoops of ice-cream. I remember countless summer meals of fresh ripe tomatoes, home-grown sweet corn, radishes, carrots, leaf lettuce with homemade dressing, the applesauce we all helped to make. I remember drinking glass after glass of Grandma's homemade lemonade mixture ... and Grandpa's home-grown apple cider. I remember sitting at that table looking out the bay window at the garden, the field of corn, the birds at the feeders, the peonies in bloom, and thinking it looked like it should be on the front cover of a magazine. Grandpa took such pride in his yard and garden. His plants and trees were his babies.

The grandchildren often designed colorful place cards for special meals and placed them where they wanted everyone to sit. Grandpa was always at the head and Grandma to his right. As the grandchildren matured, they were often allowed to write the questions that went into the passing bowl.

Dan's mother and I would spread the cardboard cutting board across the table top. We'd cut yards of fabric into the shapes that would be sewed into quilts, dresses, curtains, jackets, pillows. My mother-in-law patiently  taught me how to use my creative talents to clothe and decorate for my family and passed along that tradition to her grandchildren as well

There were countless games of *Scrabble* and *Upwords* with my father-in-law around that table. I remember clearly the time I reprimanded him in a playful tone that I took *Scrabble* very seriously. If he wanted me to play, he had to stop saying "It's just a game." and rise to the challenge! If he didn't play to win, I didn't want to waste the time. He laughed, but his game became more challenging and he often beat me. I remember countless times coaxing my mother-in-law to play with us. She never would. She said she hated games … unless it was with the babies. Then she would shine with patience and with love.

And the laughter! Whichever of my children took the seat next to Grandma would traditionally squeeze her hand repeatedly all through the solemn mealtime prayer. She would just about burst trying to hold her laughter till prayer was over. She tried so hard to be reverent and would look accusingly—and lovingly—at the culprit, as they joined in the raucous laughter.

I remember the young adults around the table getting into serious debates as Grandma and Grandpa listened and ate in silence. Mealtime in their Amish/Mennonite home life had been solemn and serious occasions. But to the children of the next generations, mealtime is and always has been a time to catch-up, to laugh, to communicate in ways that the world at large drowns out.

Oh, the memories conjured up with each stroke of oil I apply to that oak table today. The lemony fragrance evokes memories of yet another season of my life. I am taken back to childhood and my twelfth year. I am lovingly rubbing lemon oil along the grain of the new colonial maple furniture my mother purchased her first year of high school teaching in a little rural community in Ohio. She had just graduated college after struggling to maintain the Dean's List while raising three young daughters as a single parent. We had precious little furniture or possessions during the years of her education, so the new maple furniture is held in great reverence. There is an oval dining room table, four chairs, a coffee table, and a graceful rocking chair. Every weekend we girls have chores to do before play. I always love the sheen left by each stroke of oil applied. The years have flown by, and now the only remaining maple piece left in the family is the graceful rocking chair which occupies a prominent spot in the living room of her small retirement home.

Our modern worlds are very lacking in continuity and the richness of history and heritage. We are all guilty of being too encumbered by chaos, busyness, and disjointedness. Sometimes it takes the moment into quiet retreat evoked by the simple task of polishing a cherished heirloom to transport us into another world. A world of memories too pleasant to forget. Sometimes it is a song, a poem, a walk in the country, a picture, or a smell—that moment of déjà vu that reminds us of the importance of family and heritage. Being a romantic affords me a chance to appreciate, preserve, and pass on that heritage with love.

Never Miss an Opportunity to Celebrate!

Many years ago when our children were young, I had a *Come-to-Jesus* talk with Dan about the importance of remembering holidays and special occasions. It was Mother's Day, and I waited all day for some recognition and some appreciation for all I put into raising our three children. I simply couldn't believe my family, particularly my husband, would forget to honor me on this special day. I didn't say anything because I kept thinking there was a huge surprise lurking in the wings ready to be revealed at just the right time. Didn't happen.

After tucking the children into bed, I asked Dan if he remembered what day it was. He did. He simply didn't think it was a big deal. *Wrong answer. Wrong attitude.* And, in no uncertain terms, I let him know how inconsiderate he had been. But the main point I wanted to make was the message he sent to our children.

Children take their cues from the most important people in their lives, their parents. I felt that placing so little regard for a day intended to celebrate the importance of motherhood was making a statement to the children that taking the time out to honor me was not necessary. It was hurtful to me that Dan had ignored the opportunity to tell me he appreciated all I did to create our Haven of Peace. But it especially hurt that he didn't convey to our children the importance of honoring their mother. Needless to say, Dan went to bed that night feeling properly chastised and ashamed and this neglect was never repeated. In fact, we decided to celebrate as often as possible any little victory, holiday, birthday, anniversary, etc.

> *What if we stopped celebrating being busy as a measurement of importance? What if instead we celebrated how much time we had spent listening, pondering, meditating, and enjoying time with the most important people in our lives?*
>
> —**Greg McKeown,** *Essentialism*

Life can be pretty hectic and crazy and special occasions can get lost in the shuffle if careful attention isn't observed. I remember, early in our marriage, I was dumbfounded that everyone in our circle of acquaintance and our families didn't remember our anniversary. Coming from a family where divorce was rampant and there was rarely ever a wedding anniversary to celebrate, I was ecstatic that I actually *had* one. I just figured everyone else would be too. I remember Dan telling me that our special day was very special to us and not to be hurt that others didn't view it in the same regard.

Here's a little tip that keeps excitement and fun in family interaction. Never miss an opportunity to celebrate *anything*. Just for the sake of honoring one another. Mark the date on your calendar or in your schedule book or iPhone. Take the time to make the date a real celebration, if nothing more than cooking that person's favorite meal or dessert. Simply sending a physical card can say …

I love you! Or, *I care!* Or, *Congratulations!* … in a way that shows you took the time to remember.

Our oldest son, Kevin, and his wife, Teri, have seven children. That's a LOT of birthdays, special occasions, school successes, holidays, etc. So they made an agreement with their children they would do a *big* birthday celebration every other year. On the *off* year, they

Kevin and Teri and family.

do a small family dinner and gift giving. On the *on* year, they get a party with friends and family. The exception is special birth years like 10, 13, 16, and 18.

Celebrations of life should be taken seriously in a family because it gives the opportunity to show how much you care. Our son, Jared, has had many years of sobriety. Every year, on the date of his commitment to change his life, I send him a card or note to tell him I am proud of him. It's important to him, so it is important to me.

My birthday is three days before Christmas and, as a child, I had never experienced birthday parties. So for the past twenty-five years or so, Dan has made my birthday the highlight of my year by taking me to Chicago … my favorite big city … for several days to celebrate. His taking the time to treat me to this experience each year speaks volumes to me about how much he cares … and it definitely makes up for forgetting Mother's Day all those years ago!

Once I worked for a short time as the manager of a big department store. It didn't take long for me to figure out it was not a good fit (I wanted to mother everyone. *Not* manager material!) After about ten months on the job, I quit. On my last day at work, my family all celebrated in grand style, showing me how happy they were to have me back home. I felt their love.

Chicago birthday trip.

Don't make the mistake of thinking it isn't important to celebrate even the small successes and events of your life. Those traditions and special remembrances make a huge impression on others and make large deposits in your relational bank account! *No one is ever too poor to give a gift of remembrance.* Just a warm embrace or a bouquet of dandelions is sufficient if you give them with love and sincerity. And regardless of what any woman says, she is always dazzled by a gift from the heart! Never. Forget. That!

Something to think about:

What opportunities are you missing that could be turned into fun celebrations?

What *unusual* celebrations do you observe in your family that might spark an idea for others?

Are you overlooking the importance of celebrations that your spouse might wish you put at a higher priority?

Chapter Four
Putting the OM
in H-OM-E

A heart at peace gives life to the body.
—Proverbs 14:30

T hat scripture verse is written on the wall in our living room. When we bought the modest house we now live in, we had a House Blessing before we even unpacked boxes or situated the furniture. Our closest friends came to celebrate a very special day in our lives ... moving into a house we could finally buy *(through some very creative financing)*. Dan and I had spent twelve long years of being *in the desert* after losing our business, home, and cars. Our many friends had walked with us during the years we were climbing out of financial disaster. They prayed with us, encouraged us, and saw in us more than we sometimes saw in ourselves. They knew what moving into that house meant to us. It was the beginning of a new chapter full of hope, excitement, and extreme gratitude for what God had given us. It was a season ripe with anticipation and adventure. As a group, we walked through the house and anointed each doorway with oil, praying for God to use us to bless others with this great gift.

If you have been in our home, you know it isn't a mansion. In 2000, when we bought this 3000-square-foot farm house it needed a lot of enhancing and TLC. We have spent the last fifteen years making it a reflection of us. And never do we forget our promise to bless others with what we feel is our gift from a loving God. It warms our hearts every time a visitor tells us "I feel such peace in your home."

What makes a house a home? It's the love, the respect, the kindness and generosity of heart that changes a structure of concrete, wood, and nails to a place of peace, harmony, laughter and safety. A Sanctuary.

> Essential to hospitality is the open heart which results in an open house...Each of us has a home— be it a small room, a modest apartment, or a mansion—in which we can practice hospitality.
> —**Karen Burton Mains**, *Open Heart Open Home*, **1976**

The Hindus use the monosyllabic word, *OM*, to express the epitome of fulfillment. I like to think that when someone walks into our home, they feel that fulfillment in the peace they experience and the love they feel. It is our desire that others feel peace emanating from every pore of the furniture, wall hangings, every room, nook, and cranny. Putting the *OM* in *H-OM-E* turns a simple house into a cozy Sanctuary.

You don't have to have riches to create this kind of Sanctuary. Whether we lived in a small house trailer (we did for four years … 8'x42'), a foreclosure in a rough neighborhood (where our son, Jared, witnessed a robbery in progress at the gas station around the corner), or a one-hundred-year-old house that flooded three times within the first year, we made our house a home. We often had little money to decorate or renovate, but we had the desire to make the best of what we had.

The Essence of Home

Dan surprised me with a gift of a book he thought I might enjoy because it tied into what I write about these days. It's called *Happier At Home* by Gretchen Rubin. I enjoyed reading about the importance of possessions. We are all familiar with the "Money can't buy happiness!" phrase that people extol when referring to someone's materialistic attitude. Rubin agrees with that truth and so do I. However, she goes on to talk about all the things that having possessions can add to one's life.

But here's the kicker, and I was so glad Rubin points this out. There is something about having possessions that gives comfort and a sense of stability; the essence of *"being home."* Those possessions don't have to cost much. The photo on this page shows a cheap candelabra I bought at Goodwill over twenty-five years ago. Even in its prime, it probably wasn't expensive. I keep it to remind me of our struggle to keep the lights on during a time when we were building a business, and discovering where our lives would go after having lost our house and cars resulting from a business disaster. At the time, we had just uprooted and moved to Nashville and I wanted … no, I *needed* something to help me believe life was going to get better—to remind me there was elegance behind the drab and uncertainty of the now. When I saw the candelabra, I knew I had to have it even though the $12 was a huge expense to me at the time. These days, I could afford to buy a crystal and silver one if I wanted, but I still love what this one says to me—what it represents in my life.

The painting of *Girl with a Pearl Earring* by Johannes Vermeer (1632-1675) has been a long-time favorite of mine. Vermeer is one of my favorite artists, and this particular painting *speaks* to me. Once, while visiting my brother and sister-in-law, we slept in their guest bedroom and I spotted this unframed print in a corner. I practically begged Viola for it and she generously gave it to me. I brought it home and placed it in the beautiful frame I had bought at a garage sale for less than $10. I see that incredible portrait looking at me every day when I walk into my studio. It sings to my heart.

The tin of dried rose buds evokes fond memories of our daughter, Ashley Rose-Anne, who, during her high school years collected anything with roses because of her name and because they spoke to *her* heart. This whole collage of sweet possessions sits in a corner of my studio. Each piece is special to me. They make me feel a sense of peace and tether me to home in a way that sweet memories can do.

A close friend once told me that when she was interviewing a well-known interior decorator to help in redecorating her home, he walked through briskly and exclaimed that her current décor made him want to throw up. I suspect if that decorator walked through my home he would definitely fill a bucket. My home was decorated not by a professional but by the hands of love and years of memory. There isn't a room in my house that doesn't contain remembrances, souvenirs, collections, gifts, and tokens of love from family and friends. Above my computer, where I am writing this book, hangs a lovely painting. A gift to me from my first art teacher, Melanie Jackson, who convinced me I am an artist. She helped change the course of my life and I will be eternally grateful. I feel such love from her to me when I gaze at that beautiful painting.

For sure, money can't buy happiness. But the fact is, having the things around me that speak to my heart and bring a smile to my face or a tear to my eye hasn't cost much at all. To me, they are priceless. They are part of what put the *OM* in my H-OM-E.

We do not want riches, we want peace and love.
—Red Cloud (1822-1909), Oglala Lakota Chief

My friend, Dorsey, usually remarks when she walks into our home, *"I love how your house always smells."* Once when we had a group of people crowded into our living and dining areas, one lady began to weep. When asked what was wrong, she said, *"I have never felt such love in a place."* Creating a Haven of Peace doesn't just happen. It must be intentional. Loving and respectful relationships are the foundation of a peaceful home. The best way to describe how I have created the atmosphere I want in my home is to refer to the five senses. This has worked well, whether I am decorating a room in my home or an office. Perhaps this list will help you incorporate just the atmosphere you want for your own Sanctuary.

Create a Sense of Peace

SIGHT
Get rid of clutter! Clutter gives the appearance of chaos and upheaval. Creates anxiety.

Light the candles. They aren't just for company.

Grace your table with fresh flowers. Grow them or buy them.

Decorate with happy splashes of color and examples of what you want your life to *say*.

Open the curtains and shades and let the outside *come in*! Light gives energy!

Hang paintings, photos, and shadow boxes that hold special meaning to you.

SOUND

Play music or the sounds of nature *softly* in the background. It sets the tone.

Lull your children to sleep with classical or easy listening music playing in their room.

Limit TV viewing to a *minimum*.

Never place a TV in the child's or your bedroom.

Use indoor voices. Yelling and raucous behavior is relegated to outside play.

No electronic devices when riding in the car or at mealtime when one-on-one interaction can be encouraged.

Encourage sharing verbally, relating the day's adventures together. Communicating.

TOUCH

Have the home family-friendly, so there isn't anxiety over breakage or damage. Accidents happen. Expect them. Decorate in a way that *invites* picking things up and enjoying them.

Don't save the good china just for guests. Use it often. Use the cloth napkins and tablecloth. Who's more important than your family?

Buy soft sheets, blankets, and throws that invite snuggling. Create cozy spots to cuddle up.

TASTE

Bake and cook with your family. Include the children.

Some of the best conversations and sharing are done while cooking together.

The food can set the mood! Create ethnic themes and go all out enjoying a different culture. Decorate the table accordingly.

Have tea parties often. Kids love this and it provides a good time to teach manners and have an intimate moment.

SMELL

The smells from a kitchen oven create amazing memories. Bake cookies or homemade bread just before the kids come in from school. They will associate that smell with HOME.

Use scented candles and potpourri liberally.

Buy a diffuser and drop soothing essential oil in the water … like lavender or orange.

Rub yourself and your children with good smelling lotions before bedtime. This is sure to create a soothing bedtime routine that will precipitate sweet dreams.

Place sachets in your linen closet.

Something to think about:
Does your home reflect what you want it to?

If not, how can you change it within your budget?

Can you find ways to incorporate the five senses into your home or office decorating?

Can you think of other ways to incorporate each of the senses not listed here? If so, please send your suggestions to Peace@48Days.com. I would love to hear what creative ways you make your home reflect peace and love.

Chapter Five

What Doesn't Kill You Makes You Stronger

(Living the Entrepreneurial Life!)

I woke up and knew immediately that what I had just dreamed about was an apt analogy of my life as the wife of an entrepreneur. Because I had been thinking about this topic so much, and writing about it, I had to believe God was humorously handing me a visualization of what my life felt like for so many years. Perhaps, if you are the spouse of an entrepreneur, you can totally relate to this crazy dream:

> We had just purchased a new car and were taking it for a spin. The car was shaped like a bulky bullet, wide and sleek. Dan drove it up a small hill, parked in a grassy area, and got out to gain a good perusal of his new purchase. I remained in the car and, for some odd reason, was sitting in the very back of this bullet-shaped monstrosity. While Dan gazed at the car, it began to inch forward a bit and I knew that sometimes that

had happened with his tractor, so I wasn't alarmed nor was he. We just figured the brake was slipping a bit and no harm done.

The vehicle inched forward enough that it began to slowly roll down the hill. Dan just stood there like he was fascinated, watching it … and me … taking off. I began to get quite anxious. As the car picked up momentum, I began to climb from the rear across two sets of seats that had a very narrow clearing from the top of the headrests to the roof. It was arduous to push and pull myself across these seats to get to the controls. I was sweating and using contortions to accomplish the task while the car careened out of control down a busy city street. No one was in the driver's seat, so the car just plowed ahead of its own accord, gaining speed rapidly.

I wondered why the vehicle hadn't hit something yet. It seemed to follow the street and have a mind of its own. I have no idea what Dan was doing as I was in this predicament. I just knew I had to gain some control and stop that car before it ran over someone or smashed into a building. A big bus and a bridge abutment with lots of cars and people were right where I was headed. I dove to the floorboard head first and pressed my hands on the brake as hard as I could. The car came to an abrupt and screeching halt only inches from the potential collision immediately in front of me. I was in awe of how the car missed anything in its path and stopped just at the moment before total catastrophe.

And, that, my friends, is a great visualization of how I often felt living the entrepreneurial life! Scary, exhilarating, often waiting for the other shoe to drop, and yet, *usually* avoiding total disaster. (Note: I didn't say *always* avoiding total disaster!) My life has been a journey of amazing adventure, change, excitement, and growth coupled with crippling fear, confusion, frustration, and anger. I was always there with Dan in that car, navigating turns, careening downhill, and around corners, not having a clue what lay ahead of us. Yet, always having this underlying sense of calm and knowledge we were going to hit that brake just before total disaster.

There are some events I would never want to go through again. Losing our home and cars and dealing with the sense of defeat and embarrassment was not fun. But I can't deny that the years have given me an education more valuable than a certificate hanging on my wall!

I am often asked how I coped with all the financial chaos and instability. How did it affect our relationship as a couple? How did our kids handle all the change and financial strain?

For four decades, Dan has been an entrepreneur doing everything from cleaning houses to becoming a writer, speaker, and coach. He has sold cars and RVs, vocational schooling packages, telephone/address books, run a health and fitness club, an after-market automotive accessories business, and painted houses. We had months of little to no income to months when we were flying high. We had times of vacationing in style to having the electricity cut off due to our inability to pay the bill. And, what's *the worst that could happen*? Losing our home and cars? Yes, that happened too. It wasn't a pretty picture.

Bursting the Bubble

It happened in 1988, and I can still recall that sinking feeling of numbness when our failing business sold at absolute auction for pennies on the dollar and we were left in mountains of debt. It took us almost twelve years to pay it all back and be able to buy a house again, and even then we had to utilize some very creative financing. Ah yes, the joys of the entrepreneurial lifestyle! Everyone's dream …

Let me dispel a few myths:

1. **Living the entrepreneurial lifestyle is so much easier than working a traditional J-O-B.** In. Your. Dreams. Every entrepreneur I have ever run across works long, hard hours building and maintaining a business.

Most would admit that having a "real job" would be easier. Long hours, hard work, and all the responsibility is the reality.

2. **The entrepreneur has lots of freedom to work when he/she wants and leave the work behind when he/she wants.** Freedom is subjective. Struggling to grow a business and pulling every financial resource together to pay bills and start up costs diminishes the sense of freedom, often for long periods of time. The family had better be willing to sacrifice. Yes, there is freedom for flexibility, but the reality is that time taken away during the productive daytime hours usually results in late hours at night catching up.

3. **Being your own boss gives you peace and comfort in knowing you answer only to yourself.** This is actually true. You answer to yourself (and your spouse) when the bills are overdue and you are solely responsible for them. And you answer to no one else when you have to hire, fire, motivate, and oversee employees, partners, and business associates. And you get to figure out taxes, insurance, liability, P and Ls, and so on. Ah, the joys of being your own boss instead of letting someone else deal with all those details.

4. **A good education will get you where you want to go.** *Au contraire*, my friend. A good education might help in some cases and is definitely a good life experience. The entrepreneur, however, knows having personality and a willingness to work hard and long will bring you more success than most college degrees. Life is a good teacher. Failure is critical to reaching true success, and learning how to make failure work for you is essential.

Now before you peg me for a cynic, let me say, I would not trade the frustration, fear, anger, despair, and worry to have lived a different life. I am a better person for having tenaciously hung onto the kite strings of this amazing flight. And, yes, I did feel all those emotions. There were times I railed at God through prayer, and times when I simply didn't even know how to pray anymore.

So I just waited. I waited to see what would happen next. And we never starved. I learned a lot about living in the moment.

We were never homeless (although we did spend ten months with Dan's parents at one point ... with three kids, a dog, a cat, and all our possessions). Our kids didn't suffer. Their respect and love for us was never contingent on how much money we had, if we drove a fancy car, or if we vacationed on Sanibel Island or went to a park or on a hike instead.

We never had problems.
We had opportunities for solutions.
And we could get mighty creative
with figuring out the solutions!

Most importantly, our marriage didn't suffer. Back in 1968, when we vowed to one another to stick together through thick and thin, we actually took that seriously. We never considered our lives together to be too hard to reconcile. Marriage is a lot like entrepreneurialism. If one is committed, one just keeps doing everything it takes to make it work. I knew that having the attitude of, "Well, you got us into this and it is up to you to get us out!" would only make Dan feel worse than he already felt and that would accomplish nothing positive. (Ok ... I might have thought it in my head, but I didn't verbalize it!)

Were there times I wanted to yell, *"Just get a REAL job!"*? Of course there were. But realistically, I knew that working a real job would never be a fit for Dan and, if he were miserable, the family would suffer. He would have made a horrible employee. He would have had a better way to do anything he was told and would have had a hard time being a team player. So I reconciled myself to the fact he simply wasn't wired that way.

I believe in Dan. He is one of the wisest people I know, and that is a lot of what attracted me to him in the first place. I love the way his mind works.

The ideas he comes up with can sweep me away in the excitement of dreaming and planning. I want his bent towards adventure and the unknown to continue flowing into the experiences we have as a couple and a family. I think it makes all of us stronger and more interesting to be around.

Was it hard when we lost our house and didn't know where we were going next? Oh, yes, it was. But it was an experience. It wasn't our relationship. It wasn't the demise of our family. It only helped us grow wiser. Our children have benefitted from watching their parents stay united through thick and thin. A business failure should not result in relationship failure. If the proper foundation of love, integrity, and trust is established, a business failure is simply a bump in the road (Ok, sometimes a *boulder*!)

Being the wife of an entrepreneur is one of the biggest blessings of my life. I am glad I stuck through all the years of trial and error and didn't decide to chuck it all for someone more "stable and secure." I'm a better person for having been the support and stable influence that made our home a Haven of Peace and Joy. No, it wasn't all a grand ride. It wasn't all fun, and it certainly wasn't easy. But the end result has been worth it, and I can't imagine a better education for what we do today to help people discover their potential and initiate a plan to reach their goals. (www.48Days.com)

Something to think about:
Are you embracing who you are and allowing your spouse to do the same?

Can you accept how your spouse is wired and not try to force him/her into something that goes against that bent? Even if it ends poorly?

Are you committed to being supportive even when your circumstances take an unexpected voyage South?

When All Else Fails … Grab a Paintbrush!
Let me add one caveat to this topic of living with an entrepreneur that I believe should be stated clearly. Dan and I are both very capable adults. We have always known, if things got really bad financially and we didn't have money to pay the

rent or feed the kids, one of us could find something to do to tide us over till the next business idea took off. Never did we let months go by without doing something to bring in some income.

There are no secrets to success.
It is the result of preparation,
hard work, and learning from failure.
—**Colin Powell**

When I talk to a wife who is bitter, scared, and frustrated because her spouse has been working on an idea for three years while praying continually for sustenance, I want to pull my hair out. I'm all for working on building your dream, working on your idea, invention, or writing that novel you have been developing for ten years. But to pursue a dream or idea while *waiting on God* to bring food to your door, pay the rent, and support your wife and children is just plain wrong. Yes, miracles happen, but I believe, even for a miracle to occur, one has to take action for any dream or prayer to come to fruition. I have witnessed too many Christians who have used prayer as a form of spiritual procrastination … *"God hasn't released me yet to work! I'm still praying."*

Prayer is powerful. Accompanied with action, much can be accomplished. But I have talked to couples who have had years of praying over a business, a family situation, choosing a school for their child, or a possible move. They are simply waiting for God to write the correct answer in the clouds with a big Sharpie so they can know with certainty they have made the right decisions.

I cringe when I hear stories of months and years of no income. Unless you are severely handicapped, mentally or physically, there *is* work out there. If you have tried and tried to no avail, then you better start looking inward and find out what you are doing to sabotage your job search. Today there are many resources available for helping one find meaningful work, temporary work, full, or part-time work. Dan's best-selling book, *48 Days to the Work You Love* (**www.48Days.com**) has helped thousands of people find work they love, even if it is a stop-gap while building your own business.

When we found ourselves without income between business ideas, Dan and I cleaned houses. We had our five-year-old son, Kevin, go along with us because we certainly couldn't afford babysitting. He was well-behaved and the people who paid us loved having Kevin come too. In fact, Kevin often won their hearts to the point where he was given toys, a bike, treats, and lots of attention.

Dan has always been a Mr. Fix-It. His farming background gave him experience repairing, building, painting, restoring, and he became quite busy with a laundry-list of repair jobs for women whose husbands didn't have those skills. While he repaired, I cleaned. We started with cleaning our church. We got many jobs from that. The referrals happened so rapidly that very soon we simply couldn't take on any more clients. It helped tide us over during a transition period.

And, when all else failed, Dan could always find a job painting someone's house, barn, garage, or office. There were several times we paid off our rent by his painting and restoring the property we lived in. Trust me, we often had *opportunities for solutions* through the years. We just put on our thinking caps and figured out what our able bodies could handle. We knew we were employable if push came to shove. Our persistence and determination to protect our family unity by working through difficult situations together, rather than delivering ultimatums and harboring animosity, has made us more resilient and comfortable with change. In fact, we would often laugh at ourselves over yet another predicament we found ourselves in while we made plans for the next adventure. Keeping a sense of humor is a key ingredient to the entrepreneurial roller-coaster!

Something to think about:

How do you handle tough times in your family? Can you discuss some viable options for moving forward without accusations, anger, and raised voices calmly? Without placing blame and becoming a victim?

Have you set a time limit on how long you can pray about a situation before moving forward?

Can you change your thinking about having problems to *having opportunities for solutions* and see how creative you can be?

Chapter Six

Change Isn't an Option ...
It's a Given!

Change happens. Often. We live in an ever-changing world with more options and choices available to us than we can fathom. Expect change and learn to roll with it. If you don't, you will frustrate yourself and everyone around you, *especially* if you are married to a serial-entrepreneur! My entrepreneurial husband embraces change like it is the bread of life. And that is not easy for an **S** (Steadiness) personality like me.

> Change is the law of life.
> And those who look only to the past
> or present are certain to miss the future.
> **—John F. Kennedy**

Many entrepreneurs are bouncing off the walls with the need for change. I call that Entrepreneurial ADHD. Do you know there has been some great research done on the correlation of ADHD and entrepreneurialism? In a May 14, 2014, article in *Forbes Magazine*, Dr. Dale Archer, a psychiatrist and human behavior expert, wrote that many very successful and well-known entrepreneurs feel their ADHD has been the underlying boost for their success. Dr. Archer states "… it's worth noting that some of the trait's (ADHD) most common characteristics—creativity, multi-tasking, risk-taking, high energy, and even resilience—are, in fact, strengths when leveraged in the right way and in the right career." He goes on to say that those with the ADHD trait tend to thrive in times of crisis. I contend they also tend to thrive in the midst of change.

I've earned a degree in *Change Adaptation*! Our family has moved from Ohio to Kentucky to Southern California (another country!) back to Kentucky and then to Tennessee—with many moves in each of those states. We have been several kinds of Baptist, Methodist, Episcopal, Assembly of God, Charismatic, Pentecostal, non-denominational, and others I can't even remember. (And that's just since I've been married!) The children have been in private school, public school, home-schooled, and in private group classes. Sounds like we were gypsies, doesn't it? But if you ask our now grown children about their moves, their experiences, they will speak fondly of all the great family memories. Because, in reality, kids rarely hate where they are if they are genuinely loved. They get the bulk of their security from what they feel from their parents.

I see my words and actions and thoughts mirrored every day! Talk about motivation to keep growing and learning and changing!
—**Claudia Good, Author, Entrepreneurial wife and Mom to two little ones and my on-going pen-pal.**

What kid doesn't like a great adventure? And that is exactly how our family approached everything we did—with enthusiasm and a sense of adventure and excitement. I don't remember them ever becoming overly depressed in leaving their friends, neighbors, teachers, schools, playmates, church, even family members. We weren't indifferent or disconnected but, because we didn't anguish over having to leave a place or live in fear and isolation when put into a new environment, neither did our children. Life itself is a grand and on-going adventure for children. Hovering over them to *protect or shield* them from change only cripples them, makes them fearful, and overly guarded. And if we, as the parents, treat an impending change with fear and trepidation or anger, our children will express that same attitude. Granted, the older the child, the more they may resist upheaval. Being respectful of when your family needs some stability is certainly appropriate. Moving a seventeen-year-old just before her senior year of high-school will undoubtedly meet with some resistance and a lot of temper tantrums. Timing is important.

> If you don't like something, change it.
> If you can't change it, change your attitude.
> —Maya Angelou

I want to address how change can affect you adversely or positively. Because, like most things in life, how you deal with change is a *choice*. And yes, I don't like it when someone tells me this. There truly are times when I would like to wallow in misery for a little bit. Just a few days ... or weeks. But living with my adventure-seeking, change-addicted, glass half-full-and-overrunning husband who "carries his sunshine within him," I have chosen to adapt. I have chosen to include his perspective rather than dig in my heels because I've become excited about embracing life as an adventure **even though it stretches me to the max at times.**

How might change affect a family? I can tell you what it has done for us. Embracing change has given us an education you can't buy. Change has helped us grow beyond the confines of a narrow world of experience. Change has helped us be more resilient through thick and thin. Change has made us better problem solvers. (Giving us lots of opportunities for solutions!) It has helped us be more creative and adaptable to circumstances. We have grown—enlarged our scope of acceptance and tolerance. Change has exposed us to worlds we would never have known and cherished if we had not been open to the experience. And we have met and enjoyed new friends everywhere we have landed.

Of course, hindsight is usually 20/20. There were times when dealing with all the many changes in our life met with a bit of resistance from me (the steady personality, remember). There were definitely times when the changes we made were not easy or fun. Change can bring on anxiety, stress, and even grief. But how we handle change within our family has a great deal to do with how they learn to adapt. I can't stress enough that children take their cues from the adults around them. Once Dan and I made a decision to move or he wanted to start a new business venture, the two of us thoroughly talked it through. We became comfortable and in agreement before we broached the idea to the children.

Change is the only thing that opens the door
to new adventures and opportunities.
—**Dan Miller**

The roller-coaster life of financial uncertainty, frequent moves, and business changes wasn't always initially well-received by me. I learned early on not to get attached to the car I drove. I never knew when I would come home to an empty parking spot containing a cardboard box with all the contents from my current (*or ex-current*) vehicle. (Ironically, as I write this page, Dan has just had my current vehicle, which I love, detailed and put on the market to sell. He has orders to replace it with something even better or I keep it!)

Dan and I know the importance of keeping the lines of communication open, and we spend many hours talking over any new "adventure" or possibility of major change in our lives. We have to be in agreement before the change is implemented. It would be highly counter-productive not to be in agreement before forging ahead with a new experience. Keeping secrets or hiding possible areas of conflict or uncertainty simply has not been a part of our partnership. It might take some time for Dan to convince me of the value of a particular change. But it has always been hard to resist my husband's excitement each time he has approached me with a new idea. I believe in him. I want to live my life as a great adventure! His eagerness to learn and change is infectious, and I have grown and stretched and become a better and more interesting person because of our exposure to and acceptance of change. One thing I know for sure is my ability to be happy and to create a stable home for our family has never been contingent on where we live, who we knew, or even how much money we had in the bank.

Every time we moved, my challenge was to create a Haven of Peace. When we moved away from family, I found a new sense of independence that helped me grow and made me stronger and more in tune with becoming the best role model I could be. I loved decorating with the things that made our new house our home. Furniture, paintings, photos, and accessories that we were all familiar with were not all discarded each time we pulled up roots. We wanted to maintain a sense of familiarity that helped us ease into new digs.

When we landed, our Saturdays became fun family excursions of garage sales, thrift stores, and rummaging through Goodwill, excitedly gathering new items the kids would help pick out. That enabled them to *own* some responsibility for establishing a new nest. Sure, there were times when it took time for me to adjust to new surroundings and feel truly settled again, but the children didn't see it. Hard to be morose when your kids are having a great time being coached by Daddy, who is on a new crusade for entrepreneurial independence. Reflecting back, I wouldn't trade any of the great adventures (even the ones that seemed disastrous) for a more "secure," predictable life. I am a wiser, more adaptable, and stronger adult because I learned to embrace change and look at life with a broader, more open perspective. I feel certain our whole family would attest to feeling that same spirit.

Case in point:

In 1974, moving from southern Kentucky to southern California seemed like a great adventure. Kevin was four years old. Dan had just graduated with honors with his MA in Clinical Psychology. He was ready for another adventure. We bought a used pop-up camper for $845. We hooked it up to our gold, 1966 Plymouth Satellite purchased for $600 at an estate sale. (Dan describes it as "the ugliest car he ever owned.") We decided to take a tour of the country, camping along the way. We took most of the summer meandering across the states en route to Anaheim, CA, where two of Dan's sisters lived. It turned out the sisters' pastor, a psychologist, had a practice called *The Center for Human Understanding*. Doesn't that sound *so California*? This pastor quickly saw Dan's potential for being an asset to his counseling center and offered him a well-paying position there. Every new graduate's dream-come-true. And, of course, I was very excited about the prospect of being the wife of a psychologist after helping to put him through undergraduate and then graduate school. Seemed like a no-brainer for us to go back to Kentucky, pack up and move to California. We were young, adventurous, and eager for a change …

When we returned to Kentucky, we cleaned up that pop-up camper, placed fresh flowers on the table, and sold that baby for $1250 to the first looker. We used that money to move ourselves to Tustin, California, where the practice was located. It was the first and only time we lived in an apartment. We couldn't afford a house in California. Dan proudly and excitedly started his new career as a psychologist. Two months later he said, *"If I have to sit behind a desk and shrink heads for a living, I will have to be committed myself."* And he quit.

Now, put this in perspective. We had precious little money and Dan suddenly had no job. We had a four-year-old son and we had moved over two thousand miles from friends, family, and familiarity. We now lived in another country. *Seriously*. Have you ever *lived* in Southern California?

What now? Of course, my world was reeling. So … we did what any able-bodied young couple in dire straits would do. We started a cleaning business. First, we started cleaning the church we attended. It was a beautiful, little white church in Garden Grove, CA and was well-used. If I have one undeniable talent, it is making things clean and beautiful with whatever is handed to me. Pretty soon, it was common knowledge I could make a floor shine better than anyone and word spread. Other cleaning jobs came our way and, before long, we had more houses to clean and small home repairs to do than we could handle and we had to stop taking on new clients.

Did I have a hard time adjusting to this turn of events? Well, let's just say it was not a highlight of our great marriage. I was all set to be the wife of a psychologist. After all, I had worked hard to help put him through years of schooling. Now I could relax and enjoy a life of leisure and financial gain, right? *Not exactly*. I certainly had some frustrations and anxiety for awhile, but with Dan's continual positive attitude and sense of adventure, and the support of new friends, my misgivings were short-lived and we began to have fun. We would take Kevin to work with us and the clients loved him. He was given toys, candy, ice-cream, and lots of attention.

Did I have thoughts of moving back to more familiar surroundings? Oh, yes. I remember crying on that first Christmas away from family and friends and lamenting that it couldn't possibly be Christmas because I was in shorts and a halter top! Back then, we could hardly afford the cost of a long-distance phone call, much less a trek across the country. But we made the most of it. We made lots of new friends through our church and had great California experiences. Before long, Dan was offered a job working in a friend's car business selling cars. The owner and his wife were quickly becoming our very dear friends and with Dan's love of cars, this was an awesome fit. So I tried to get my mind around being the wife of a used-car salesman rather than a psychologist. Oh, yes, I certainly had mastered Change Adaptation.

Dan worked in that business for almost three years. He made more money than he could have possibly made as a fledgling psychologist. He helped start an RV rental business as another source of income. We had amazing vacations and fun life experiences with Irene and Jerry (owners of Halls Auto Sales), who became very dear to us and remain so to this day.

Irene and Jerry Hall with us at baby dedication ceremony for our son, Jared in 1978.

But the story gets better … We were young, in our early thirties. Many of my new California friends were having babies, and I got the bug to have another child. Jared was born in Anaheim in 1978. Kevin was a seven-year-old when he got a new sibling. Having two small children made us think seriously about where we wanted to raise them. We were pretty sure it wasn't going to be in Southern California. Irene and Jerry, Dan and I would take our motorhomes to Lake Tahoe and sit in our camp chairs discussing how much we hated the escalating traffic congestion, smog, and fast pace of living in Southern California. We would "escape" almost every weekend to the desert to dream and talk about what we wanted to do with our lives. We all decided to move, and by then the four of us had enough money to do so. Irene and Jerry had spent much of their lives in California. Their families were there. Our families were in Ohio. We gave ourselves a couple weeks of prayer and exploration to make a decision as to where we would go. We figured we had the whole country to look at, but we decided to return to Kentucky because we had loved that part of the country and had friends and familiarity there. Irene and Jerry decided to move to Northern California where they started a new business and reside today.

So, once again we made the long move across the country. Dan and Kevin (eight and a half years old by then) rode in the NOT air-conditioned U-Haul truck full of our belongings with windows down singing "Take It Easy" by the Eagles among other crazy songs. I followed behind in my huge Cadillac Eldorado (fun days!) with Jared in an infant seat, our cat, Brandi, and my dear aunt, who had flown out to help with the move. At least we had air conditioning and comfort!

We had the U-Haul rented for five days. We took three days to make the trip and parked the truck in my sister's driveway for two days while we searched for a new home. Now mind you, we had left California with no housing arrangements for when we got back to Kentucky and no idea what we would do for income. I knew this was going to be *one heck of an adventure!* We couldn't find anything we could afford to rent, so we approached the owner of a house near my sister's house that had been on the market for sale and asked if they would consider renting to us. They agreed and we moved in, returned the U-Haul at the allotted time, and started to address what we would do to earn a living. Now, remember we had packed all our belongings into a U-Haul truck. We'd moved our family across the country from California to Kentucky, searched for a place to live, and moved all in the span of five days. It pains me to even think about it now.

We were running out of money so we had to think fast. We both agreed I should stay home with the boys. We considered everything from a diaper service (seriously!) … to teaching at the University. Dan had taught Psych 101 as a graduate assistant at Western Kentucky University during his graduate school days. But by then, the entrepreneurial bug was so entrenched in Dan's mind that it was hard for him to wrap his mind around the limited income and time constraints teaching would afford him. We mulled over many possibilities. It was like we had a clean slate on which to paint our future.

Each day you awake to a new canvas.
You get to choose the tools you will use
and what you want to create!

One day, Dan mentioned he had been fascinated watching the guys who would come to the car dealership and apply pinstriping to the vehicles on the lot. It was popular in the late '70s and the early '80s to trick out your vehicle with stripes, huge decals, etc. (Remember the eagle that covered the entire hood of the Pontiac Trans Am Firebird of that era)? So, we bought an older van and had it painted. We created a logo that said *Auto Appeal*, a name my sister, Margie, came up with after many hours of brainstorming. Dan bought a small amount of inventory, and a new business was born. Of course, one small detail was missing. Dan had never actually *applied* any decorative striping or huge decals in his life. He had *observed* others doing it in Southern California and just assumed he would be able to do it. No sweat. (Dan is fond of saying when confronted with an opportunity for a solution … *No step for a stepper!*)

Keep in mind this is a true story! The *very first* dealership he went to excitedly gave him five cars to stripe without batting an eye. Dan politely thanked the owner and said he had a very busy schedule that day, but he would return the next day to do the job. He promptly came home and spent the rest of the day in the bathroom. He was sick with anxiety. He had just committed to doing something he had never done. He knew he had to dive into it as if he were a professional with a lot of experience. With much encouragement from Kevin and me, he returned the next day to the dealership. While the owner watched him and carried on a congenial conversation, Dan laid out and applied beautiful and creative designs on all the vehicles *and* received his first check. He was ecstatic. Incidentally that business became very successful, largely due to Dan's integrity and his desire to be the best automotive accessory installer in the area. We soon were able to rent a building with a workbay from which he could install sunroofs, stereo systems, window tinting, and many after-market accessories. (I won't even go into all the anxiety he experienced when he had to cut a hole in the roof of a brand new vehicle and install a sunroof!) We eventually acquired several *Auto Appeal* vans and I would often be at the office/garage to help with customers, paperwork, billing, etc. When our youngest child, Ashley, was born, we would take her with us and she would sleep on the floor behind my desk. We were building a business together and, unbeknown to us then, getting the education to help others in the future.

So many great memories and experiences had happened during those previous three years in California. The friendship with Irene and Jerry has lasted nearly forty years. Although I didn't become the wife of a psychologist, the work experience Dan had buying and selling cars prepared him for this new business in Kentucky. It thrived and supported us well as we had our third child and became entrenched in establishing a new life in a beautiful home we could now afford to buy. I firmly believe that every new place we landed helped propel us to new heights on our road to success. Not just monetarily, but educationally and emotionally.

Frequently I get asked questions like this:

"Weren't you scared?"

"Did you ask him to get a real job while you settled down from the move?"

"Don't you feel this kind of lifestyle is a bit risky?"

Was I scared? Well, I suppose there was a part of me that was a tad fearful. However, it all seemed like a big adventure at the time, and I had seen Dan pull us through other tough and uncertain situations. Surely he would do it again.

If I even came close to mentioning he get a real job, he would turn pale and his stomach would tie up in knots. It was such a foreign concept to him, and he knew he would hate it. I knew not to push that button because, if he was miserable, I knew the rest of our family would also suffer. We weren't starving ... yet ... and I knew if push came to shove, Dan would find temporary work to put food on the table. Dan took his role in our family seriously. He wouldn't risk our family's welfare.

> Risk is putting the deed to your house on the table in Vegas.
> The way to avoid risk is to put a plan into motion.
> —**Dan Miller**

Dan couldn't see himself doing the same thing day in and day out with a set schedule and no flexibility in income. He knew he had to do something creative and, yes, we were both apprehensive and really too naïve to look at all the impracticalities of what we were doing. (Sometimes naïveté works to one's advantage!) Ironically, he labored twice as hard trying to make his business work than he would have if he had had a "real job" where he would follow the rules and get a regular paycheck. But he was happy. So we all were happy.

I knew if Dan was to be the breadwinner of the family, I wanted him to be happy in whatever he did. I knew that I wanted to be there to support and love him and create a Haven of Peace for him to come home to each night. Creating that safe environment for him became *my* career. In looking at it with this perspective, I felt better about me being a stay-at-home mom when most of the world would dictate that I should be bringing in income too. We both felt that my career as a mom and supportive wife was an integral part of whether or not Dan would be successful in his entrepreneurial endeavors.

At the Corner of If and Then …

> *The one thing I am most proud of with my husband is that no matter what he does, he strives to be the best he can possibly be. He works hard to be at the top of his game … Of course, then when he gets to the top of his game, he decides this isn't any fun anymore, and he is ready to move on to the next adventure.*
>
> —**Irene Hall**, wife of a serial entrepreneur

My long-time best friend, Irene (wife of Jerry, owner of Hall's Auto Sales where Dan worked), and I have often laughed about how one day we would write a book called *IF* about living with an entrepreneur. I couldn't count how many times in all of Dan's entrepreneurial endeavors he has said "IF this happens ... then this will happen ...!" And I would get caught up in his dreams of bigger and better and his plans for our getting on top of things. Irene experienced the same with Jerry. The four of us had fun dreaming and planning together back in the late 1970s. All these years later, Irene and I frequently talk about how the IF and THEN words intersect in our husband's conversations and plans. It's a serious malady! And it is the mantra of most any serial entrepreneur. The projections always look ten times better than the reality and it's a darn good thing people like Jerry and Dan have wives like Irene and me! But what if that isn't the case? What if you have a spouse who is not at all supportive? Let's talk about that ...

Chapter Seven

Are you a
Debbie Downer?

D an recorded a podcast about the importance of not spending a lot of time with negative people. He talked about his three-hour rule where he might spend three hours a year with negative friends but certainly not three days or three weeks on a vacation. He said he knew he was broaching a subject that left an elephant in the room. And, sure enough, he began getting a plethora of emails and comments saying, *"What if that negative person is my spouse?"* Ouch! He also heard from many who remarked, *"I am that negative person. What can I do to change?"*

Hope keeps the fires of inspiration fueling the
embers of the entrepreneurial and creative mind.

One person commented:

These are scary times we live in and I almost feel hopeless like America is over. Obamacare and other things scare me. It seems as if economic activity is slowing down. With the pending conflict between religious and gay rights, I also fear that this country is going to abolish religious freedom. I fear we are the nation mentioned in Revelations which is going to experience Judgment and ultimately fall. In short, I feel like America is almost over. I wonder how you deal with the uncertainty of these times.

I love how Dan responded to this message. He pointed out a perspective that changes the reality of the above comment to a different reality he and I have chosen to adopt:

I'm confident, if you eliminated listening to talk radio, stopped watching TV, and never read a newspaper for thirty days, you would see your optimism soar. The negative issues shoved at us because negativism gets ratings give us a very unrealistic view of our country today. Talking to real people about their dreams, seeing my grandchildren experimenting with their entrepreneurial businesses, being involved in my local community in developing areas of beauty, and spending time just enjoying life with Joanne, makes me more excited about the next ten years than I've ever been in my life.

It is a puzzle to me why our society seems to thrive on tabloid news that is full of all the reasons we are *going to hell in a hand basket!* Years ago, Dan and I adopted the practice of rarely listening to the daily news. We no longer subscribe to a newspaper and we pick carefully the magazines and books we allow into our home. The only regular television we ever watch is *Wheel of Fortune*. It is a good way to chill a bit after a long day of writing, interviews, etc. When it is over, we switch to a music channel and actually engage in conversation and togetherness in the evening. *This is a choice we have made to maintain the peace and tranquility of our home.*

But what if you live, day in and day out, with someone who is continually negative? What if every time you have a new idea, your spouse knocks the wind out of your sails with all the reasons why it won't work or is a stupid idea?

Here is a list of common concerns and comments we hear from spouses:

- We can't afford to take a risk right now.
- We don't have the money.
- You don't have the time.
- It can't be done like that.
- Someone else is already doing that.
- You don't know where to begin.
- Better be safe than sorry.
- You're not that good.
- You've failed in your last three ideas—why would this one be different?
- You're just a dreamer—not a doer.
- You don't have the credentials.
- You're not a leader.
- You can't compete with Dave Ramsey, Michael Hyatt, Pat Flynn, or John Lee Dumas.
- You're too old—you're too young.
- You don't have the right degree.

Dan and I did a follow-up podcast specifically on this issue because this is a very real *opportunity for a solution.* You can easily leave a group of friends or relatives that are negative, limiting your exposure. But if the negative person is your spouse, you need to understand where this might be coming from and how you can best deal with it.

First, let me list a few reasons why someone might tend to see the negative side of some situations:

1. **Low self-esteem**: Putting others down or seeing the dark sides of an issue are often ways a person gives him/herself a false sense of power and control. They feel better about themselves if they view others as inferior. By viewing their circumstances negatively, they find comfort in being the victim.

2. **Don't have a good grasp of who they are:** They have little insight into personal awareness and have difficulty with introspection because they don't want to face what they may find. Introspection takes a lot of time and emotional energy and is often quite painful.

3. **Anger, hostility, resentment:** Often this anger comes from past experience; family baggage, abuse, neglect, etc. Often these people are great at "stuffing" their true feelings and need a lot of validation.

4. **Manipulation:** Another false sense of power and control. Often these individuals mask their true feelings and criticism with laughter and sarcasm to make it more palatable for the recipient. They think this "sugar coats" their barbs and negativity.

5. **Distrust of others:** Often there are genuine reasons for this distrust, such as betrayal, neglect, non-validation, and being let down so many times it is hard for them to trust anyone or any circumstance.

6. **Jealousy and envy:** Sometimes it is the people closest to us who want us to stay as we are. If they see their spouse/partner/friend getting ahead while they are feeling stuck and miserable, they feel better about themselves if everyone around them feels the same, validating their misery.

I have mentioned in previous chapters the importance of communicating clearly with your spouse. I know I personally have a tendency to think negatively. I can easily couch my thought process in terms of *gathering the facts* and *being realistic*. Trust me, when you live with a consummate dreamer/visionary, it is sometimes necessary to bring Dan back to Earth (reality)! Understanding each other's personality is so important. I can easily get caught up in Dan's dreams and grand ideas. I have learned to just listen. I do the same with my children. They, too, are dreamers, entrepreneurs, and visionaries. I listen. *A lot*. Often if I simply wait, I find the newest idea has changed anyway, so I take my friend, Gail Hyatt's advice and "*Wait to worry!*"

Author Peter Drucker says that the most important thing in communication is hearing what *isn't* being said. That is a powerful statement and one that needs to be continually embraced in a relationship. If you focus on hearing the underlying cause for fear, anxiety, or distrust in the negativity, you can be better equipped to handle objections.

In recapping the podcast we did on dealing with negativity, Dan gave these five solutions which may help you in better dealing with a spouse who is more than a bit skeptical:

1. **Recognize "security" is not just money in the bank.** Emotional security includes affirmation, support, and encouragement.
2. **Acknowledge different personality styles.** There are not "good or bad," "right or wrong" styles—just different. See the added value of having different perspectives.
3. **Look for the *fear* behind the negativity.** Have you let the person down at previous times? Recognize not hitting a goal is not always a *failure*. It may be the very step required for your ultimate success.
4. **Listen more, talk less.** Listen to nonverbal clues and watch body language. Let your actions convince your spouse rather than your words. Sometimes just validating your spouse's concerns are enough to turn the fear into interest.

Something to think about:
What are you feeding into your mind daily that might contribute to the negativity in your attitude?

If you see yourself as a negative person, are you open to exploring why? Are you open to trying to see the positive in your circumstances and not always jumping to the negative possibilities?

What/who are your children watching that might feed into their looking at life negatively?

How much time are you spending with negative people?

Do you actively seek out people who are performing at a level you wish to attain?

You Wanna Do *WHAT*?!

If you don't have a strong relationship with your spouse and children, chances are you will get a negative reaction to telling that spouse you want to quit your "real job" and launch a business that is going to further risk jeopardizing that trust factor. Even coming up with a solid business plan and great projections are no guarantee a new business will be successful. Sometimes even the best-laid plans go awry. I am here to tell you adamantly if your partner isn't supportive from the onset, chances are your relationship is going to go South after you've experienced a few failures. Pointing fingers, laying blame, and saying, *"I TOLD you so!"* is a real relationship killer.

In 2001, Thomas J. Stanley wrote the very popular book, *The Millionaire Mind*. He polled many decamillionaires and discovered that nearly one-half of the respondents indicated their success was largely due to having a supportive spouse. Stanley stressed the importance of having integrity in the home and wrote, *"You cannot expect your spouse to be supportive if you lie and cheat. Your spouse and your children have many, many opportunities to observe your behavior. It's not enough to say you are honest or merely attend religious services each week. You have to be a role model of integrity for your spouse, your children, and all others. If you are, your spouse will probably support you through good times and bad, during thin years and plump years"* (*The Millionaire Mind*, Thomas J. Stanley, 2001, Andrews McMeel Publishing).

Living the entrepreneurial life requires hard work and sacrifice and is definitely not for everyone. However, I am keenly aware that many people think the grass is greener on the other side when they start to feel burned-out or taken advantage of in a traditional job. On the outside, it seems quite appealing to be your own boss, be able to take off a day when you want to, or accumulate more money because you aren't salaried.

I'm going to assume the entrepreneur-*wanna-be* is the husband. So one day, with a big smile on your face, you go to your wife and say, *"Honey, I'm going to quit my job and start my own business!"* Here are some pointers on what you had better have in place if you are thinking along those lines:

1. You'd better be ready to present a good business plan with realistic projections.
2. You'd better be willing to talk through her fears, concerns, and initial shock—*validating* her and not ridiculing, belittling, or accusing her of not trusting you. Watch your body language and your tone of voice, both of which speak LOUDLY, and can totally negate the words pouring out of your mouth.
3. You'd better not quit your real job till you feel your spouse is comfortable with moving ahead and you have some traction and income with the new business.
4. You'd better be ready to communicate your desires in a way that includes her. Knowing what is going on is important to a spouse who may be timid about the future. Knowing what is happening even when it may not be good news is better than being left in the dark and speculating disaster.
5. You'd better allay her fears concerning how the bills are going to be paid. Perhaps you can assure her you won't quit your real job till you have sufficient income coming into the new business. Or reassure her you have large enough savings to help through lean times that are inevitable while building new savings.

6. Go slowly. Plan carefully. Include her if appropriate, but don't force her to fill positions in the business for which she is not well-suited or she dislikes.

7. And most importantly, if your spouse is in total disagreement with you on what you are attempting to do, recognize this may *not* be the best time to forge ahead. Also, be aware there may be other underlying issues for her mistrust or disapproval. It may take some time to build the trust needed to step out into unknown territory.

What Can You Control?

> Security is mostly a superstition.
> It does not exist in nature,
> nor do the children of men
> as a whole experience it.
> Avoiding danger is no safer
> in the long run than outright exposure.
> Life is either a daring adventure or nothing.
>
> **—Helen Keller**

Consider the words of Stephen Covey in *7 Habits of Highly Effective People*.

Instead of reacting to or worrying about conditions over which they have little or no control, proactive people focus their time and energy on things they can control. The problems, challenges, and opportunities we face fall into two areas—Circle of Concern and Circle of Influence

Proactive people focus their efforts on their Circle of Influence. They work on the things they can do something about: health, children, problems at work. Reactive people focus their efforts in the Circle of

Concern—things over which they have little or no control: the national debt, terrorism, the weather. Gaining an awareness of the areas in which we expend our energies is a giant step in becoming proactive.

Covey talks about how our lives don't just happen. We design them by our attitudes, our choices. We all want "security"—especially within the family circle. But security is a very elusive concept and certainly differs from person to person.

In a recent interview, I was asked if I sometimes longed for all the attention and support I gave to Dan. My response was that I would not have wanted to be as effusive in my attentiveness to his needs if he had not reciprocated. Having a one-sided relationship of giving gets pretty old as resentment builds and feelings get hurt. (Reread the prologue) Dan and I have always been open with one another on what we fear, what we desire in our home, and in our relationship; what is and is not working. For all the many ways I support Dan in this marriage, he does the same for me. He has always encouraged me to be the best ME I can be. (I will discuss this more in a bit.) And when I haven't been able to figure out what that is, he helps me. He encourages me and he shows he is proud of me for who I am. That's monumental in establishing trust and respect. I'm sure he could write a book about my support, love, and encouragement that allowed us to have the lifestyle we created.

True and lasting love manifests itself in bringing out the best in one another.

A few years ago, I gave Dan a metal wall decoration bearing the single word INTEGRITY. He felt honored, and it hangs prominently in his office. Integrity is the best word I could possibly use to describe how he treats me, our children, his clients, friends, and anyone with whom he comes in contact. Because he is a man of integrity, I trust Dan to make the best decision he knows how to make with the information he has at the time. I trust Dan to make good choices for our relationship and for our family. I trust him to consider how every decision he makes affects more people than just himself. We are a tight unit and, although each of us has our own identity, dreams, and goals, we are always mindful how our decisions and actions affect the other. We have built a strong foundation of trust. And trust is often the most important component to embracing change and uncertainty in one's future. I know without doubt Dan would never make a major decision based solely on his own desire and without including me in the process. Why would he *crap in his own nest* (Dan's words)?

Never lose sight of the fact that the most important yardstick of your success will be how you treat other people.
—Barbara Bush

What's the *Worst* That Can Happen?

I can't tell you how many times I have posed that question to an audience who are fearful of stepping out into a new business venture. "What's the worst that can happen?" Invariably, the concerns center on losing a house, cars, their possessions, and their "stuff." They are concerned about losing face in the community: "What will other people think?"

I'm here to tell you those issues are definitely *not* the worst that can happen. The worst is losing your relationship, your trust, and support of one another. Believe me, it is easier to replace a house than a broken marriage. Ultimately, the willingness to support a spouse unconditionally will usually override any fear of insecurity, undergirding the spirit of adventure.

In all the years of our own search for success, I often attended seminars and conferences *with* Dan. I like to think he included me because he enjoyed my company, but I suspect he had a hidden agenda. He knew that if I heard the motivational speakers and authors, I would get caught up in the energy and excitement *he* was experiencing. My better understanding of what it takes to achieve success would nudge out all the negative fear and anxiety. And he was right. I *would* get excited. I would see potential I didn't realize was possible. I have seen this same thing happen to attendees of our own conferences who brought a spouse *just along for the ride.* And they got so caught up in the possibilities and the excitement of creatively living life differently that they have been inspired to pursue careers, write books, or start a blog themselves.

It's hard to be an Eeyore when you live with a Tigger!

Admittedly, having heard many speakers, attended dozens of conferences, listened to many podcasts, and devoured many motivational books have all led me to a desire to do more with my life. Tapping into all those resources gave me the confidence to write my own books, to stand in front of audiences and share what I know, and to be a mentor to many who want to create an adventure instead of just a life. I have become a better-rounded and more interesting person to be around. And I have become less concerned about what might happen if we lose our possessions because of a potential business disaster. If I had to go back to living in a little 8' by 42' trailer like we started out in back in 1968, I could do it in a heartbeat.

I love what our lifestyle affords us now, but I know, beyond a doubt, what is more important than all we have accumulated. More important than our bank accounts, more important than our beautiful home and land, more important than our business … is a deep and abiding love for one another and our Haven of Peace which can be established even in a small trailer.

Chapter Eight

A Tragedy or
an Education?

Don't you sometimes wish you could know what the future holds when dealing with change? Our son, Jared, once wrote in an email to me from his home in Africa that he no longer feared hardship. He said he had learned many times over that God always has a plan waiting to unfold, and it typically has a much better ending than he could possibly predict on his own. Wise words from a then thirty-year-old.

Dan is a strong personality and he can usually accomplish what he sets out to do. Sometimes when God seemingly closes a door, Dan has been known to kick it in and forge ahead anyway. Kick in enough doors and eventually someone says, "yes." I can still picture the two of us lying crosswise on the bed in our cute little home in Bowling Green, Kentucky, over thirty years ago. Dan was explaining to me that a friend of ours wanted to sell his business, a big health club with several thousand members. He wanted Dan to buy it. I laughed. Seriously.

We had a great business going with Auto Appeal. We had built it up to bring in a good income and our lives were going smoothly (which should have been a red flag that things were about to change). We lived in a new home, the children were healthy and happy, and we were living the dream. Why would we need to buy a health club? Especially since I have always been of the conviction that people who love to exercise are masochistic! Neither one of us had ever even stepped one foot into a health club, so my initial reaction was to think he was joking. But Dan was convinced he could make it work, and since we had some great employees at Auto Appeal, he felt he could run both places at the same time. The more he talked, the more excited he became, and his enthusiasm, determination and ability to convince me made me have a lapse in sanity. I wasn't thrilled with the idea but told him if he could pull it off, I would learn to live with it and be there for him. That's all it took. He was off with the speed of lightning to the local bank that promptly turned him down for the loan. So he went to another bank. And then another. He had stopped after the seventh bank turn-down and then he approached several friends who invested in this great adventure! Dan worked hard for several years to build the membership, fix up the place, and make it a nice club. Once he got established, he was then able to get lines of credit from the bank. But it didn't take long before we both agreed that trying to run two businesses simultaneously was more than he could handle … particularly when those two businesses were diametrically different—aftermarket auto accessory installation vs. health and fitness club—with very different skills, clientele, and daily interactions. Before long, he sold Auto Appeal to a trusted employee and concentrated on making the health club prosper. We bought a new home and settled into a comfortable lifestyle that ended up being much shorter than we expected.

Several years later, banking practices had a big overhaul and notes that Dan had signed with the business as collateral were called in unexpectedly. We were in a big hurt. We didn't have the financial resources to pay these notes and were behind with business taxes to the IRS. Dan put the club up for sale but had no takers. The IRS and the bank were breathing down his neck relentlessly, so he decided to put the club up for absolute auction, figuring if we just broke even we would be ok.

I'll never forget the day of that auction. It was a nightmare I don't ever care to repeat. The feeling of terror and out-of-body numbness that came with the lowering of the gavel. The auctioneer yelling, *"SOLD!"* when the selling price was a mere fraction of the hundreds of thousands of dollars we had in debt, made me feel nauseous. It was more than frightening. I think I walked around totally numb for days. I couldn't even begin to imagine the fear Dan had in knowing he had gotten us into this fiasco and we were now faced with losing everything we had worked so hard to attain.

There were days when we clung to each other out of fear and desperation, and there were days when we felt distant from one another because we were too afraid and angry to face the truth. Our son, Kevin, attended the auction and was old enough to know a little of how devastating this was to us financially. He says he can remember that day vividly. He hurt for us.

> You can't climb the ladder of success
> dressed in the costume of failure.
> —**Zig Ziglar**

I knew I had to maintain sanity for the sake of our children. I knew I had to continue to create peace and a safe haven for them and for Dan. It was my job and my responsibility and I took that seriously. Although I seemed to be walking in a fog and hardly able to comprehend the severity of our situation, I knew Dan was struggling with his own sense of failure trying to hold our lives together as he cleaned out the club and made his exit.

The kids and I came up with a plan to give him time to wind down a bit when he got home each day before pouncing on him with our own needs, excitement, and adventures. I would often have a bathtub of water waiting with soft music and candles so he could relax and pull himself together before he faced the family with a cheerful countenance. The children enjoyed helping me prepare this special gift for their Dad.

Dan and I had a choice to make during those dark days. We could be angry and create distance and more stress or we could pull together and make our family strong through the difficult days ahead. I could say, *"I told you this was a bad idea!"* or I could accept Dan did what he thought best for our family at the time, but it didn't turn out the way we had hoped. So … lesson learned. Here are a few key business principles for you:

Rule #1. **Never go into a business you know nothing about.**
Rule #2. **Never put all your assets in said business, so you lose it all if things go South!**
Rule #3. **Never mess with the IRS!**
Rule #4. **Reread Rule #1.**

But here is a solid truth to close out this story. Looking back to the events all those years ago that were seemingly so "disastrous" and could easily have torn our family apart, I can't think of a richer, more appropriate education for what those days allowed us to do.

Ultimately we put our house on the market and sold it ourselves before the IRS could take it. We sold our vehicles because the IRS demanded money. Dan borrowed a $400 broken-down car from a car dealer friend so he could drive to New York City to speak at a club industry convention one last time. We needed the money too much to decline, and he had made the commitment to go. That car leaked oil so badly he had to continually stop to add more. The windows wouldn't work and he couldn't lock it … which in NY is not a good thing. The radio didn't work in the car so Dan took a little portable tape player with him and played motivational tapes … Zig Ziglar, Brian Tracy, Earl Nightingale, Dale Carnegie … trying to lift his spirits and feed positive thinking into his brain.

When Plan A Fails

How did I manage to keep my sanity while losing our house, cars, and "stuff?" I won't say it was easy. And I won't deny that I had moments of anger, frustration, and despair … toward my husband and toward God. Can't say I'm particularly proud of that, but I am being honest here. When a woman's security is threatened … when her sense of peace is shaken, her emotions run the gamut of extremes. I think the younger you are, the more fear you may experience. *I was only forty years old when we lost our beautiful house, our cars, and our "stuff." Still young enough to envision a future that was full of unknowns. Still young enough to really grieve over what others would think. Of course, I was also naïve enough to hope that we would surely recover from this loss in a short amount of time. But that recovery period took us twelve years. A long time to hang on to hope. A long time to *wait on God.*

*Ironically, many people say this about being older; that a business failure can be the worst in this stage of life. Again, it's all about perspective. I look back now and see how all the pieces fit together and needed to happen for the next piece to fit. So my fear level is much less now than when I was younger. Taking Jared's attitude that God usually has a better plan anyway helps to curb any fear I have now.

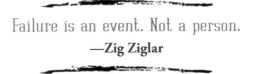

Failure is an event. Not a person.
—Zig Ziglar

At the time of this "disaster," Dan was the head of the Small Business Development Center through our local Chamber of Commerce. Suddenly he went from being a successful businessman in the community to having lost his home; having the IRS putting liens on anything we owned; and feeling a profound sense of being a total failure. This was not the image he wanted to portray to the people who looked up to him as a leader in the business community. But surprisingly, when he told the Chamber he needed to resign and why, he was told they wouldn't accept his resignation. They pointed out that NOW he could really relate to others trying to start businesses and encountering all the hardships, hard work, and frustration involved. Now he had the experience to help others in a very real way … through his own struggles. And, through the years, we have found this to be so true. Our experience is the reality of business. It happens sometimes. And one thing we know and believe adamantly is that *failure is an event, not a person.* And a failed experience can be the best education for moving forward, helping others, and creating a new beginning that might turn out even better than Plan A.

However, having people understand, sympathize, and love us through all the aftermath of that devastating loss didn't pay the bills. It didn't appease the creditors who called daily (before caller ID) and didn't give us any glimpse into a more promising future. So the questions often arose, "What are we going to do next?" And "How can we EVER pay off this debt?" We had three children ages 17, 10, and 7. Three mouths to feed and clothe beside ourselves. We had an attorney friend who strongly advised us to declare bankruptcy which would help us get out from under a lot of the debt. We simply couldn't bring ourselves to do that. Dan had accrued the debt in good faith, and he would fulfill that obligation if the merchants would just hang in there with us. Most agreed to do so.

Dan soon found a sales job that took us to Nashville, TN, only an hour south from where we had lived in Kentucky. We were relieved to move to a new city because we felt the need to start over in many ways. But it was not easy. We had to get really creative about finding a place to live. Through our church, we heard of someone who wanted to move to our area and needed someone to live in their Nashville home till summer when they would put it on the market. It was not in the nicest or safest part of Nashville but was a blessing to us in this transition. We rented there for six months while we got on our feet and got acclimated to our new city home. Our entertainment included watching the police regularly come to our neighbor's house for drug busts and cleaning up the mess when the ceiling caved in in the downstairs of the house where we were living. Fun times.

> Success is not final, failure is not fatal:
> it is the courage to continue that counts.
> **—Winston Churchill.**

During the next few years, Dan worked several sales positions to put food on our table and pay the rent. I homeschooled the younger two children and our oldest was pursuing a successful bicycle racing career so he was traveling out west and overseas. We moved often trying to find affordable housing and keep our heads above water. At one point, we even moved back to rural Ohio to live in the upstairs of Dan's parent's country home while Dan checked opportunities for work there and we tried to save some money. We lived there eight months but ended up going back to Tennessee and renting again. Through those years, we couldn't buy a home because of IRS tax liens against our credit.

It was a hard twelve years financially. But it was ripe with opportunities to learn, grow, and believe that one day we would be out from under this cloud.

Plan B Is Better

When we moved to Nashville, we immediately became involved in a huge non-denominational church. In no time, we started teaching a Sunday School class on Career-Life Management 101 (we thought that sounded very academic!). We certainly had experience in what not to do as well as pointers on how to start, manage, and grow a small business. The class kept growing. People came from other churches to attend, We soon found we were missing worship service because we were being asked to counsel so many people who came to the class. Soon we moved the class from Sunday mornings to Monday nights, teaching eight sessions on career issues, job search, and creative income which rotated all year. The classes were open to the community and we were asked by another church to do the same program there. Little by little we developed handouts that turned into notebooks and then turned into spiral-bound booklets, which then turned into cassette tapes and more products.

We actually began building the business we have today from that fledgling Sunday school class ... which we would never have been led to if not for the "disaster" that happened to us in Bowling Green. Life is a grand puzzle and often we have no concept at all of where each puzzle piece will lead us to form the perfect Plan B or maybe even Plan C.

From that Sunday school class, and from the business failure all those years ago, came the curriculum and material that formed 48Days, LLC. I have no way of knowing how many thousands of lives have been changed, businesses started, careers changed, books written, marriages saved ... all from what would appear to have been a perceived failure and low point in our lives. Dan has since written many books, created a social networking community with over fifteen thousand members, and spoken out on business/career and life issues for over twenty-five years now. And we have been unified in our family goals, supporting one another all the way. I know beyond a doubt, none of our current success would have resulted if we had given up when our world came crashing down over two decades ago. It hasn't been an easy road to success. Success doesn't work that way. It takes determination and hard work to achieve any worthwhile goal.

The Puzzle of Life

Life is complicated to be sure. In her bestselling book *The Artist's Way*, Julia Cameron talks about synchronicity. Some call it coincidence or serendipity or luck. Cameron says, "We call it anything but what it is— the hand of God, or good, activated by our own hand when we act in behalf of our truest dreams, when we commit to our own soul" (*The Artist's Way*, Tarcher/Putnam, 1992, by Julia Cameron, pg. 64).

I believe our faith should be acted upon. Our lives don't just evolve without our active participation. God ordains and we have the responsibility to fulfill His Plan for us. Embracing this philosophy, I like to think my life is much like a giant and intricate jigsaw puzzle and all the zillions of tiny pieces fit together in a way that, bit-by-bit, makes sense. Sometimes a huge pattern of pieces fits together almost miraculously and it makes sense that each piece has to be there to form that section. One small piece can't be left out or the patterns don't go together properly.

Some of the pieces are crazy—vague and seemingly void of clues as to where they might fit in but, given time and patience, those pieces become intricate links to connect the other pieces together. *No piece can be left out and no piece is insignificant.*

There are cornerstone pieces to the puzzle—pivotal points in life—birth and childhood, adolescence and coming of age, marriage and/or career, old age and death—the four corners of the puzzle. The outer frame between those corners is all the pivotal events that connect those four pillars, the necessary pieces that make us human beings with complicated, involved steps to maturity and aging. The four corners are the hinges to the doorways which open to all the stages of our lives.

It's beautiful if you look at life this way. It makes sense. We need all the pieces in the middle to help us learn and grow, cope and survive—those inner pieces make up our inner being. We are complex. We need each piece of the puzzle to connect to the next piece. If we leave out a piece here and there, we miss important steps in putting our lives together. There is a spiritual and physical balance that is necessary to connect all the parts.

Sometimes we get on a roll and all the puzzle pieces fit together really well in one section and we know we have "listened" to our Creator, our directive, well. We have shunned discouragement and anger, frustration and defeat, and forged on till we made the right choices and placed the pieces in proper sequence, and now it all makes sense. What a wonderful feeling it is to look at that section of the puzzle with delight. To know that perseverance, dedication, and keeping your eyes on the goal have paid off in the beauty of a well-developing puzzle portrait so beautiful that it is obvious it is *divinely ordained.*

Now that section is complete; it is time to conquer another, then another ... until one day we look at the puzzle and see the clarity of life that we could never have dreamed would appear. We think back on how those pieces fit together and are amazed at the intricacy and all the events, people and experiences that went into the making of this divine creation ... *one solitary life ...*

Lost ... or Found?

Sometimes it is very difficult to keep one's own sense of self while being married to an entrepreneur with a strong personality. When asked if I ever felt I put my own career goals on hold, I have no problem responding that I always knew my primary career was to be dedicated to the marriage and the family I had chosen. I loved being a wife and mother and I made it my career. Did I ever feel I got lost in the shuffle? That question always evokes a lot of angst in me because it is not easy to answer.

Early in our marriage, Dan made it clear he didn't expect me to be a clone of him or to put him on a pedestal from which he would eventually topple. He has always encouraged me to be *ME*. Admittedly, he is the stronger personality, but his desire has never been to dominate or control. Remember in an earlier chapter when I talked about personality styles? When I said that any strength can become a weakness when overused? Dan figured out early on, if he came on too strong, he could hurt my feelings, undermine our relationship, and dominate. He knew that was not the relationship he desired.

From our beginning, I wanted to create a home full of peace and love; the two things I craved most and often didn't feel growing up. I sought out mentors from our church whose home life I admired. I watched, listened, and quickly adapted the tools to having an environment Dan and our children were happy to come home to. When we started having children, I continued to learn from others around me and from books and tapes on how to create a home where everyone had peace and felt love. It has been my life's mission.

However, I did have a point in midlife when I began to realize I needed some help. I was no longer sure of who I was and where my life was going. I call it *The Ugly Year*.

The Ugly Year

I got lost somewhere along the way. It was gradual, or maybe I never really knew enough about who I was to even have a beginning from which to stray. I think you can spend years, even decades, just being what you think you are *supposed* to be, doing what you think you are *supposed* to do. I'm very good at being malleable and am definitely a people pleaser. I spent decades making everyone happy and comfortable; paving the way for their success, never taking the time to wonder who I really was?

I loved being a supportive wife, mother, and friend. Nurturing comes easily for me and, I suspect, my own lack of being adequately nurtured from childhood played a huge part in my continual quest to satisfy that need in everyone I came across. Especially my family; in my home.

But then I turned fifty. For me, it was an ugly number. It was a blatant reminder of how I was aging and a look in the mirror was further proof. I used to be a model: slim, unblemished, perky, and pretty. What happened to that young thing? I was depressed. Really depressed. I was having physical problems with numbness, weakness, and fogginess that scared me, and before long I was almost unable to walk. My right side had gone numb and weak from the top of my scalp to my toes. I went to five different doctors who all confirmed I had Multiple Sclerosis. So along with the depression, I dealt with chronic fatigue, weakness, and confusion, with big doses of fear for what my future might hold.

But that wasn't all. I was experiencing a bad case of empty nest syndrome. Ashley was off to college—my last child to leave home. I felt like I had gone to work one morning and been instructed to clean out my desk because I was fired! Being Mom was my career, the main objective was to be the BEST ... MOM ... EVER!

It was an ugly year for me. But, I know now, it was the beginning of a journey that changed my life dramatically.

I remember like it was yesterday, sitting with Dan, weeping and asking him, "What do I do now? My children no longer need me. I have been downsized! Or fired!" (I spoke in terms I knew he would understand.) Have you ever had "head knowledge" you couldn't get your heart to accept?

Dan patiently pointed out to me that I simply needed to take my gifts and shift them to a different focus. I exclaimed that I didn't even know what my gifts *were. I had just been a mom and wife!* And I had done a darn good job of it! I could help others see their gifts and value, but I had trouble seeing my own. Dan helped me recognize my worth as a nurturer and pointed out that he had often witnessed how friends and clients gained new hope and belief in themselves through my words of encouragement. I had led them to make significant changes in their lives.

I began to get an insight into my innate temperament and discovered I didn't need to think my job was over; I needed to gain a new perspective. I could use my love of nurturing and loving people through other avenues and through our business. I would always be Mom. My children would not be leaving my life, just my home. And that was a *good* thing. My love of helping others began to transfer to clients, women's groups, and a prison ministry, all of which allowed me to become *Mom* to many. I got involved in a mentoring program for ex-felons and have spent many years being *Momma* to a young mother who was desperately in need of a hand up upon release from prison. I began to see where my strengths in encouraging, leading, and loving others were applicable in many areas other than just at home

But I still felt the need to do something just for me that was not the normal embracing of my innate abilities. Something outside the box. Something to stretch me and be just mine and was not contingent on making someone else happy. I saw an advertisement in the local newspaper for a drawing class. I had never drawn. I didn't think I was at all artistic, although I did crave beauty around me and had worked hard to create a lovely home for my family. I decided, on a whim, to sign up for the class. It was hard and it definitely stretched me. But that class led to the discovery of the artist inside just waiting to be unleashed.

I remained in that class for thirteen wonderfully creative years. The strength, self-confidence, and discovery I gleaned prompted me to write four children's books and a book on creativity for adults. I become a speaker, a leader, began hosting a weekly art class at our Sanctuary, to do podcasts, blogs, and a host of other creative endeavors. I have entered art shows, won blue ribbons, and have even sold a few pieces of my work. I discovered parts of me that I had never taken the time to explore before and that have radically enhanced my life.

Would the quest for finding *me* have happened if I had not had that ugly year when I was forced to face myself—to dig inside and find parts of me that I didn't know existed? Hard to say, but I am forever grateful for the discoveries made as a result. I am forever grateful to an art teacher, Melanie Jackson, who encouraged me to express myself in ways that tested my patience and abilities but made me a better person. I am forever grateful to a husband who knew I had been tapping into my gifts even before I knew for sure.

Often unearthing the beauty in your life requires digging through the ugly and uncomfortable. What is revealed is the authentic YOU that lies dormant, waiting to spring to life when brought to the surface.

And, yes, I still have MS. It is relapsing and remitting, so I go for years at a time basically asymptomatic. I have learned to take better care of myself and to not allow MS to define who I am. Only a few people know I sometimes have physical struggles. I have learned to appreciate every day I am healthy and unencumbered by fatigue, confusion, weakness, and depression. I have learned to seize every adventure and opportunity for increasing my awareness, learning new skills, and enjoying God's amazing world. And to be grateful in all things.

Life is full of surprises. Turning fifty was a turning point in my life that brought light out of darkness and gave me the courage to forge ahead with confidence. The ugly days spurred me on to greater success and happiness than I could ever have predicted, and revealed a new world to be embraced.

So I ask you, did I really get lost along the way or did I continue on the path of self-discovery to reveal parts of me that were ready to be birthed for a new season of my life? I think the answer is pretty clear and I am thankful for *The Ugly Year* that pushed me into new territory and an incredible new season of my life.

Something to think about:

You do have a choice in what direction you want your life to take. What might you be incubating that is just waiting to be unleashed? Are you taking opportunities to explore other parts of you that stretch and teach? Can you expect greatness to come from ugliness?

Chapter Nine

And They Lived Happily Ever After ...

I have a small ceramic tile on the shelf just above my kitchen sink that reminds me daily of one of my principle tenets in life. It says: "And they lived happily ever after ..." My sister, Margie, gave me that little tile for Christmas one year—I am sure she has no idea how meaningful that gift is to me. It is a daily reminder of a choice I make to enjoy life to the fullest. I know I have God on my side. I know I have a loving husband and three amazing children to encourage me along the way. I know each day I wake I can choose to make this a good day or I can choose to wallow in self-pity, depression, anger, and myriad other negative emotions. I choose not to go that route every day.

As children, we believe innocently and sincerely that we can live happily ever after. Why, along the way of life, do we become so disillusioned and cynical that we no longer believe it is possible to have a happy ending? Or why do some get so caught up in the process of attaining happiness we fail to see the beauty of life on the journey?

In doing prison ministry, I hear stories that break my heart. I see lives that have never been properly nurtured, loved, encouraged, or given a shred of hope. However, I am amazed at the laughter and joy those who are incarcerated can find in a simple piece of scripture, a new friendship, singing a joyful song, or clinging to a light at the end of the tunnel.

I hear stories about impoverished countries where the poorest of the poor find happiness in the simplicity of their lives. They find solace in worshiping a God many of us take for granted. They hold on to each other and find happiness in spite of their circumstances.

I am a firm believer that happiness begins inside one's head and inside one's home and family. I know there are those who have no family or whose family is so messed up it seems impossible to find joy in the dysfunction. However, I have also seen how one can break away from those influences, make a decided effort to create their own happiness, and still live happily ever after. It is always a choice.

I take life seriously. I believe in being productive and hard working. I used to think I took it too seriously and it bothered me a great deal. I felt a real need to embrace life rather than just endure life. I took action to find resources to help me learn to travel in the right direction. I read books to help me see life with new eyes. I saw movies that impacted me positively. I made a practice of incorporating fun and laughter into our days as a family and as a wife. I am not willing to settle for mediocrity. I want to know when I pass from this mortal flesh that I have no regrets about what I have missed. So I choose to embrace life with gusto and happiness.

Something to think about:

What determines your happiness?

Do you believe you can live a happy life in spite of your circumstances?

Who Will Think of Me?

I was cleaning out and redecorating a bedroom. While sorting through the debris that had been collecting for years in drawers and cupboards, I kept running across items that would trigger a memory of some family event. They evoked a chuckle or a groan or an occasional "Oh, yuk!" as I tossed the item in the waste basket. My mind often tends to meander down a one-way sentimental and romantic path.

While tossing trash and placing sentimental memorabilia in boxes to keep (probably till the next cleaning and redecorating frenzy when I am a little more ready to part with it), I kept wondering what would trigger a thought of pleasant memories in the heads of my children and grandchildren long after I am gone. Now I realize to some this may seem like a morbid or silly thought, but it kept passing through my mind. Finally, I had to disentangle myself from the plastic drop cloth my feet had adhered to from the paint I had dripped all over the floor, maneuver around the furniture pulled into the middle of the room, and gingerly run into my office for paper and pen to jot down my thoughts before they left my brain just as quickly as they had arrived.

What will trigger a thought of me one day that will make my daughter sit down, a gentle smile on her face and a tear in her eye? What will elicit a chuckle from one of my sons or a grandchild? It may be a very simple object or a picture. It may be a fragrance or a melody. But I pray I will one day be the instrument of a moment's memorable pleasure for someone I love and have impacted in a positive way.

One summer, I was slathered in perspiration, mud, and grass stains as I helped my husband construct a large rock waterfall in the front of our house. Our work put me in a cloud of adrenaline. Soon I was contentedly creating a rock garden: strategically placing stones from around our acreage in just the right spots to give the new waterfall the appearance of having been in that very spot for years. I was lost in thought when I realized I was in the land of *Déjà vu*. A smile crossed my face as I recalled the rock gardens my mother and I had created when I was a young child in the hills of Kentucky. Where we lived was very shaded and grass was impossible to grow. We couldn't afford pretty flowers, but we could make rock gardens to enhance the beauty of the hillside, transplanting wildflowers, ferns, and mosses from the woods nearby. Finding and placing the rocks and stones in just the right spots was, to us, like putting together a jigsaw puzzle ... fun, challenging, and very gratifying when it was finally finished. It was a sweet recollection of the past that threw a cloak of warm memory over me as I toiled in my yard decades later.

I live in the South. It is a rare home in this area that doesn't know the comforting smell of white beans and ham simmering on the stove. A familiar Southern comfort food that, for me, evokes fond memories of my tiny, wrinkled grandmother who cooked this dish several times a week for her family. She always included sweet cornbread with this menu, and I would make myself a grand treat by crumbling warm cornbread into a glass of whole milk and eating it with a spoon as my dessert.

Another comfort food that brings an endearing thought to mind is hot oatmeal. I still remember twenty-five years ago when my dear Aunt Becky visited our home to spend time helping us with our new son, Jared. I was so thrilled with having an extra pair of hands to help with a new baby and his older brother, Kevin, who had been the center of attention for seven years prior.

One morning, Aunt Becky got up early to take care of Jared for me so I could get some much-needed rest. I soon was aroused from my slumber by loud and anguished mutterings from the living room. Seems Aunt Becky had Jared all bundled up in one arm and was carrying a bottle of warmed formula and baby oatmeal to the rocking chair to sit. Somehow, the lid came off the top of the bottle and next thing she knew she had dumped the entire contents down the inside of our coveted

Fisher stereo sitting next to the rocking chair. She was standing there aghast when I entered the room. We laughed as the two of us tried, not very successfully, to extricate the gooey concoction from the innards of the stereo. Miraculously, Dan still listens to music blaring on that same stereo receiver now in our barn all these years later.

I have inherited the antique wooden sewing table that my mother-in-law, Clara, sewed on for decades. She sewed garments for me, my children, and many for herself through the years. I watched her, helped her, and learned so much. She taught Ashley how to sew and we still think of Grandma Clara every time either of us sits at that sewing table in my bedroom. Clara is there with us ... she always will be. We had lots of wonderful laughs sitting over that sewing table. We shed a few tears, too.

My home is pieced together like an intricate quilt with all the memories of events and people and stories stitched together with love and familiarity I hope never to replace simply because it is worn or out of fashion. My home is a composite of all the loved ones in my life who have made my life so full. Sometimes I reflect in joy. Sometimes a tear comes to my eye. Sometimes I experience a profound longing for just a few more precious moments with the loved ones I have lost.

One day, Ashley and I were riding in my car and she popped in one of her favorite CDs. She looked over at me with a big grin on her face and eagerly said, *"Momma, you gotta hear this!"*

The CD was the soundtrack from the movie *O Brother, Where Art Thou?* I listened lovingly as I heard the very familiar strains of "You are my sunshine, my only sunshine. You make me happy when skies are gray!"

"Remember, Momma? You used to sing that to me all the time when I was little."

I remembered all right. I had to choke back the tears as I smiled and flashed back many years. I marveled something seemingly insignificant in my eyes was a memory that would linger forever in the heart of my grown up child as she tenderly holds her own child in her arms and sings ...

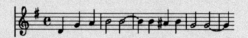

"You are my sunshine, my only sunshine.
You make me happy when skies are gray!"

Chapter Ten

The End ... or Is It?

Our children are grown and married. Dan and I are often at home alone with no one to talk to but each other. That is a frightening thought to many couples facing a new season of togetherness without children. Often, each parent has been so immersed in their own lives they have forgotten how to act like a couple again. They have drifted apart and the anticipation of the inevitable "empty nest" approaching can create uncertainty and anxiety about what this new season is going to bring. I have witnessed many marriages dissolve because there is no longer any feeling of connection or tenderness. This is especially true if they have created a child-centered home.

Let's skip the "should have done" and the "if only" and discuss some action steps to regaining that closeness and intimacy you had when you were young and in love.

Make Time. Time to discuss your fear openly that you no longer connect and might be drifting apart. This is *NOT* easy. Having a serious talk about the disappointment and frustrations you feel in your relationship is never easy. But it is essential to moving on. If you can't lay the cards on the table and talk like adults, then get a counselor to mediate and help. If you think you are too "mature" to take your problems to a counselor, you are fooling yourself. You are actually being childish, insecure, and ignorant. This should not be a time to fight. Discussing why you feel a disconnect should not be accusatory or hateful. A counselor can help mediate if you have trouble communicating without throwing something! I promise if you make time to discuss your concerns you will be taking an important step in the right direction!

Work to Regain the Romance. Schedule trips together. Quit using work or the kids or your important meetings as an excuse. Gary Smalley wrote a book in 1989 called *Love is a Decision*. Read it. Unless you are in an abusive relationship, it is time to rethink your priorities. Your relationship should take precedent. Life-after-kids can be the most amazing season ever. Take a cruise. Take weekend road trips. Do things you used to love to do together. Go on a second honeymoon. Don't allow the kids/grandkids to derail you by disrespecting your need/desire to have this freedom.

Find Common Interests. Dan and I used to go to car races together and, because he loves cars, we go to car shows and exhibits together whenever one is in town. Take a class together. Something that interests you both. Garden together or read a good book and discuss it. Take a ballroom dancing class. We did this a few years ago and even though there were often weeks we felt we had a dozen reasons not to go to class, we were always glad we did. Honestly, I don't think it is possible to take a dance class together and not laugh at yourselves!

Find New Friends. If you don't have any good friends who are couples you like to hang out with, find some new ones. Look for marriages you would like to emulate. Organize game nights or a dinner club with couples who have strong, healthy marriages and watch what they do. Refrain from interacting with negative people. If you are complaining that you can't find new friends, you aren't serious about looking. Don't wait for them to show up at your door. Take action.

Learn to Touch. It thrills me, even after decades of marriage, to have Dan put his arm around me or hold my hand. When we walk, when we are in a group or if we are alone in the car, Dan and I touch a lot. It may sound hokey, but that small gesture of "I care" does a lot to create intimacy in a relationship. And the more you touch, the more you close the gap that occurs when you have a disconnect. And don't forget the importance of a healthy and enjoyable sex life. Don't be content with just having a roommate.

Play Games Together. All those family game nights made us aware of how important it is to PLAY together. To challenge one another in a friendly game, to laugh together at the silly mistakes, losses, and craziness is *life* to a relationship. Dan and I still play at least one card game every day. It makes us laugh and enjoy one another's company while taking a break to de-stress and be in the moment.

Find Yourself. If you no longer know who you are, what you want to accomplish in life, and/or what excites you, perhaps it is time to work on yourself. I have found, personally, the times I have been discontent or angry with Dan often have the root of discontent with myself. Once I became more aware of what my strengths and passions were, I got more excited about living life to the fullest. It made my conversations with Dan more lively and interesting. And made me less dependent on him to provide my happiness. I am serious about this. Be the best that *YOU* can be and you will be surprised how your spouse will respond.

Keep Your Sense of Humor. Don't take life so seriously you forget how to laugh at yourself. It seems the older we get, the more Dan and I have to cover each other's backs. Rather than calling each other "forgetful" or "crazy," we simply laugh at ourselves and are grateful we have one another. Turn your foibles into funny. Laughter creates a positive emotional connection that should be practiced daily.

It's never too late for a new beginning.
—Dan Miller, author and love of my life

Living a full life is undoubtedly everyone's goal. I have never heard anyone say, "I want to have broken relationships, be mediocre and die lonely!" A successful business, the finest house, the flashiest cars, and clothes will not fill that hole in one's heart for good relationships; people who love them and they love in return.

Creating a Haven of Peace for your family can change your family tree. It can give you the comfort of knowing you have people who love you unconditionally, and can provide a Sanctuary for immunity, security, and safety. It takes a concerted effort to establish this in a home. But you can do it. You now have many tools and examples from reading these pages. I have no doubt you can add your own suggestions and experiences. And in your continual efforts to create your own Haven of Peace, I have no doubt you, too, can live *Happily Ever After …*

The Kids Speak Out

(None of my children read this manuscript before I asked them to write a little about what impressed them most in their upbringing. None of them read what his/her siblings wrote before I received all their responses. This is from their heart and from their memories.)

Peace Has Few Rules,
but Some
Definite Boundaries
By Kevin Daniel Miller

A s I sat thinking about what impacted me most growing up in our home, I was drawn to thinking about my children's friends now … and where their heartbreak is with their parents.

Mom and Dad were reasonable and rational in regards to life and me. They treated me with respect. They welcomed and expected my input, and they included me in their life and thoughts.

I see so many kids today who seem to have this gulf between "us and the adults." They seem to come from two different worlds. I never felt that.

Which is why, on many a Friday night when my friends would call to ask me to join them in some activity, I'd often ask Mom to answer the phone and give an excuse for me. I would rather stay home and watch a movie or play *Scrabble* with my parents.

On that same note of being reasonable and rational, two things stand out with respect to creating peace:

1. The family business and finances were often tumultuous and I was aware of the stress involved. I wasn't shielded from reality. I knew why we were driving a Cadillac one year and a jalopy the next. I appreciated being included in real life. Again, it made me feel valued and respected. Shielding kids from reality seldom does them a favor. It makes them weak, not strong.
2. Life, love, and peace prevailed, no matter our financial state. It grew my faith in going after things and not being fearful in regards to the circumstances.

As a guy with admitted authority issues, who loathes being confined by boundaries, we really don't have any "rules" in our home. We are incredibly lenient with our kids.

However, this is all corralled by one massive, absolute rule: Your freedom is curtailed and stricter boundaries are enforced if/when you infringe on someone else's well being. We demand respect. Non-negotiable.

This was how I was raised. When other kids had curfews and rules and fear of report cards and grades, I was free and at peace. As long as I gave respect. No curfew, but let Mom know where I was. Grades weren't paramount, as long as I was learning and growing in other areas. My input was desired and accepted, as long as I sought out and accepted others.

When your kid is 100% free with no
boundaries, that means they are stepping
all over someone else's boundaries.

When kids run absolutely wild and have little respect for anyone or thoughts for another soul other than themselves, parents live for the end of the day. They live for the time when the kids will just go to sleep and give them a moment of peace. Thus, the recent best-selling book that, while somewhat funny, is tragically sad, *Go the "F" To Sleep* by Adam Mansbach. That seems to sum up the overall parental feeling these days. This is not reasonable. It's not rational. And it doesn't create peace. The number one principle in my experience as the son of the parents I have, and now, as the father to my own seven … Is *respect; of yourself, of others and of the world around you.*

Follow Kevin at
www.agentkmiller.com
and listen to him host
the weekly Ziglar Show.

Relationships
Trumped Everything
By Jared Nathan (Miller) Angaza

I remember very vividly when mom and dad brought us together to write our family mission statement. It was hand-written on a piece of paper, laminated, and stuck on the wall. I must have read it hundreds of times throughout the years. It wasn't a fleeting thought. It formed our ethos and influenced our beliefs. It's engrained in my psyche and has profoundly influenced my perspective and priorities as a husband, father, and activist.

We were not financially wealthy. We didn't have much in the way of materials things. We had something far more valuable. The love and genuine joy in our home were palpable. The perspective, priorities, and lifestyle of our family are well-known among friends and family. Our home has always been the safe place for anyone needing solace or refuge.

Benevolence wasn't a chore or obligation. It was the natural result of the philosophy our family fostered. There was no judgment in our home. There were no grudges. In our home, you were safe. You were nurtured and cared for. We were shown love and grace rather than judgment and condemnation. Consequently, our home was always full of visitors; always abounding with the energy of all walks of life. From stray dogs to stray kids to burned out CEOs. Everyone was equal. Everyone was showered with love.

I believe a perspective of oneness and love is paramount to peace. Each of us is born with this perspective. Over time, society attempts to replace these elements with fear and division. But in our home, that was never allowed. *Relationships trumped everything.* Every action was founded on a desire to foster connection and harmony.

Our parents exemplified love and inspired us to do the same. That example continues to ripple out through each of our lives. It's at the core of the identity of our family. Our parent's mission to make our home a Haven of Peace is a legacy that continues to impact countless lives across the globe. But it started in our home, with two parents that believed that no matter the circumstances, love always wins. That, to me, is the essence of a "Haven of Peace."

Follow Jared at
www.jaredangaza.com.

Our World Is a School
By Ashley Rose-Anne Miller Logsdon

The things that resonate with me most from my childhood are two words—growth and respect. In our household, it was a given that respect was to be shared by everyone and everything. You respect our things, you respect all feelings, and you respect all people no matter their age. In our generation, there was a lot of authoritarian parenting going on, and I remember voicing my frustrations to my parents about my friends who were so "rebellious and unruly." I would go into their homes and the backtalk from the kids wasn't what so shocked me; it was the overall disregard by the parents on the idea of mutual respect. The parents would demand respect from their children yet show no respect for them. They didn't stop to listen, didn't acknowledge the feelings going on with their child, and didn't show any trust in them as being competent human beings. *When their expectation was that of an incompetent child, that is exactly what their child became.*

My parents validated me, honored my individuality, and respected me as a significant voice in our family. They treated my emotional needs at five, fifteen, twenty-five, and beyond with the same level of importance. Even if it was a dramatic "Monica said she wasn't my friend anymore!" or a lost puppy love, my parents listened to me and gave merit to my emotions. Regardless of the level of importance deemed in their adult worlds, in my world, what was happening to me *was* significant, and they allowed me to feel it and walked with me through it.

They taught me to always keep growing. They instilled in me a love for learning and a fascination with discovering something new. With my gamut of schooling (home-school, public, private, group classes), I never believed that learning was confined to a classroom. I saw my parents grow with me, learn with me, and always be open to changing their ways. They gave me grace in my growth and I saw in them the same open-mindedness to change and learn better ways to live and love throughout their own lives with parenting, marriage, business, and more.

I value these things so much and have so incorporated it into my own family. From the time my girls could walk and talk, they have known our top two family mottos: Respect all things, and the world is our school. We can show respect even if a viewpoint is different from our own; we can show love despite hate in the world; we can show consideration and honor to our environment and everything in it.

I unschool our children (yes, Unschooling is a form of education. Look it up.) As they get older, we intend on world traveling. We intend them to not only learn the stories, but to actually see and experience the sights, sounds, and overall culture of being in the places about which we study. We never stop learning, and our children have no animosity with that word. "School" is simply living fully with an open mind, and educating ourselves about this beautiful world we live in, learning more about it every day.

I am thankful for the family I came from and the family I am now creating. I am thankful to raise children who are confident in the powerful little women they are—at ages two, five, and eight. I know as they grow physically, they will always be growing mentally with their openness and love for life.

Creating a "Haven of Peace" started in my childhood and has spread to every person we come across. What stirs within our own souls can leave such a powerful footprint on everyone else we meet and, in turn, can truly change the world.

Follow Ashley and her unschooling adventures at
www.mamasaysnamaste.com.

About the Author

Joanne and Dan Miller live on nine acres in Franklin, TN. They have three happily married children who are populating their own village with fourteen children between them ... all of whom have been largely home-schooled without the influence of television. And they are actually happy, well-adjusted, and not social misfits!

Joanne is an artist, speaker, and author. She has written *Be Your Finest Art* with co-author/artist Dorsey McHugh and has authored four children's books in the *I Wanna' Be*™ series based on children's individual personalities, and *What If It Were Possible?* to be released in November, 2015.

Joanne and Dan hold conferences in their Sanctuary, speak at events together, and can be reached through www.48Days.com.

Email Joanne at Peace@48Days.com.
(I would love to hear from you!)

For the audio version of *Creating a Haven of Peace*, go to www.48Days.com/product. In her own voice, Joanne reads the book in its entirety and adds her own humor and side notes!

Be Your Finest Art is a **picture book for grown-ups.**

Not just a book about art, but a piece of art in itself. With the feel of aesthetic beauty, this book is full of examples of people who express their creativity in ways beyond holding a paint brush, singing a song or creating a poem.

Believing and teaching that we are all creative, Joanne Miller and Dorsey McHugh will show you examples of how engaging the right brain enables one to improve physical and emotional health, create stronger relationships and open new pathways of learning. They want you to rediscover the joy of childhood abandon and reclaim your authenticity. And through it all, they want you to relearn how to play!

The Be Your Finest Art Journal is a great accompaniment to your Be Your Finest Art book or a stand-alone gift for anyone who wants to stretch their right brain. Included are exercises to "wake" up your senses and your ability to experience your world with greater clarity and excitement and blank journal pages for you to doodle, think and create.

http://www.48days.com/byfa/

More From Joanne Fairchild Miller

I Wanna Be®...series

The I Wanna Be® Series of children's books validates a child's uniqueness with fun illustrations and lyrical prose. These books are great tools to help parents and young children cope with budding expressions of independence.

Based on the grandchildren of Dan and Joanne Miller, each book focuses on a different personality style that makes each child extra special.

www.48Days.com/store/iwannabe

Printed in the USA
CPSIA information can be obtained
at www.ICGtesting.com
JSHW012012140824
68134JS00024B/2383

9 781630 477714